Embellishments

Other Books Available from Chilton

Robbie Fanning, Series Editor

Contemporary Quilting Series

Appliqué the Ann Boyce Way, by Ann Boyce
Contemporary Quilting Techniques, by Pat Cairns
Fast Patch, by Anita Hallock
Fourteen Easy Baby Quilts, by Margaret Dittman
Machine-Quilted Jackets, Vests, and Coats, by Nancy Moore
Pictorial Quilts, by Carolyn Vosburg Hall
Precision Pieced Quilts Using the Foundation Method, by Jane Hall and Dixie Haywood
The Quilter's Guide to Rotary Cutting, by Donna Poster
Quilts by the Slice, by Beckie Olson
Scrap Quilts Using Fast Patch, by Anita Hallock
Speed-Cut Quilts, by Donna Poster
Super Simple Quilts, by Kathleen Eaton
Teach Yourself Machine Piecing and Quilting, by Debra Wagner
Three-Dimensional Appliqué, by Jodie Davis

Craft Kaleidoscope Series

Fabric Painting Made Easy, by Nancy Ward
How to Make Cloth Books for Children, by Anne Pellowski

Creative Machine Arts Series

ABCs of Serging, by Tammy Young and Lori Bottom
The Button Lover's Book, by Marilyn Green
Claire Shaeffer's Fabric Sewing Guide

The Complete Book of Machine Embroidery, by Robbie and Tony Fanning
Creative Nurseries Illustrated, by Debra Terry and Juli Plooster
Creative Serging Illustrated, by Pati Palmer, Gail Brown, and Sue Green
Distinctive Serger Gifts and Crafts, by Naomi Baker and Tammy Young
The Fabric Lover's Scrapbook, by Margaret Dittman
Friendship Quilts by Hand and Machine, by Carolyn Vosburg Hall
Gifts Galore, by Jane Warnick and Jackie Dodson
How to Make Soft Jewelry, by Jackie Dodson
Innovative Serging, by Gail Brown and Tammy Young
Innovative Sewing, by Gail Brown and Tammy Young
Owner's Guide to Sewing Machines, Sergers, and Knitting Machines, by Gale Grigg Hazen
Petite Pizzazz, by Barb Griffin
Putting on the Glitz, by Sandra L. Hatch and Ann Boyce
Serged Garments in Minutes, by Tammy Young and Naomi Baker
Sew Sensational Gifts, by Naomi Baker and Tammy Young
Sew, Serge, Press, by Jan Saunders
Sewing and Collecting Vintage Fashions, by Eileen MacIntosh
Simply Serge Any Fabric, by Naomi Baker and Tammy Young
Soft Gardens: Make Flowers with Your Sewing Machine, by Yvonne Perez-Collins
Twenty Easy Machine-Made Rugs, by Jackie Dodson

Know Your Sewing Machine Series, by Jackie Dodson

Know Your Bernina, second edition
Know Your Brother, with Jane Warnick
Know Your Elna, with Carol Ahles
Know Your New Home, with Judi Cull and Vicki Lyn Hastings
Know Your Pfaff, with Audrey Griese
Know Your Sewing Machine
Know Your Singer
Know Your Viking, with Jan Saunders
Know Your White, with Jan Saunders

Know Your Serger Series, by Tammy Young and Naomi Baker

Know Your baby lock
Know Your Pfaff Hobbylock
Know Your Serger
Know Your White Superlock

Star Wear Series

Sweatshirts with Style, by Mary Mulari

Teach Yourself to Sew Better Series, by Jan Saunders

A Step-by-Step Guide to Your Bernina
A Step-by-Step Guide to Your New Home
A Step-by-Step Guide to Your Sewing Machine
A Step-by-Step Guide to Your Viking

Linda Fry Kenzle

Embellishments

ADDING GLAMOUR TO GARMENTS

CHILTON BOOK COMPANY

Radnor, Pennsylvania

Photography by Robert Fogt; illustrations by the author
All clothing pictured designed by the author
Designed by Tracy Baldwin

The Penny Storm quote that appears after the Introduction is taken from *Functions
of Dress* and used by permission from Prentice-Hall, Englewood Cliffs, New Jersey.

Portions of this book first appeared in *Stylepages* and *Threads and Fibers*, published
from 1984 to 1987. Smocking first appeared in *By Machine Monographs—Smocking*,
Third Coast Press, Crystal Lake, IL, 1984.

Thanks to everyone who helped me make this book the best it could be: Don Carlo,
Joshua Kenzle, Robbie Fanning, Susan Clarey, Susan Keller, Sandy Eliot, Lily West,
Dylan Neslik, Kate Witherspoon, Bob Fogt, Natalie Goldberg, and Joy Chapman.
Thanks also to all of the companies that generously donated supplies for my experi-
mentation.

On the front cover: "In Full Bloom" chintz vest, featuring a confetti mosaics collar
(see Chapter 3), details created with slick paint and shisha mirrors (see Chapter 2),
and a hand-wound closure (see Chapter 4)

Manufactured in the United States of America

Library of Congress Cataloging-in-Publication Data

Kenzle, Linda Fry.
    Embellishments : adding glamour to garments / Linda Fry Kenzle.
        p.   cm.
    Includes index.
    ISBN 0-8019-8478-5
    1. Clothing and dress.   2. Textile crafts.   3. Fancy work.
    I. Title.
    TT560.k46   1993
    646.2—dc20
                                                    93-27082
                                                    CIP

1 2 3 4 5 6 7 8 9 0   2 1 0 9 8 7 6 5 4 3

Thank you to the foremothers
who spoke in cloth with a
needle before they were
allowed to use a pen, and to
my contemporaries who step
out on a limb as often as
possible.

Contents

Foreword

In a recent quilt guild neighborhood meeting, I admired a woman's unconventional use of appliqué at each joining of the pieced blocks. She burst out laughing. "That was to cover the hole where they join. I didn't want to set in the shape, so I appliquéd it over the hole."

It is this same inventiveness that flavors Linda Fry Kenzle's book. She conveys a marvelous sense of play with fabric, thread, beads, and buttons that is engaging. It makes you want to run for the cloth and DO!

I especially like her sense of freedom without guilt. You don't have to finish the inside before you wear it, she tells us. Use that old fabric you never liked to practice painting and stamping. If you don't like what you've made, cut it up and use parts in appliqué.

Linda's book inaugurates a new series for Chilton, called StarWear. We all carry a secret star around inside us; it's time to let it out, through our clothes. Linda's book has exactly the right spirit for this series. And I am particularly pleased to be associated with her, because I have admired her work since the early 1980s, when she published an inspiring sewing journal called *Stylepages*.

As I age, I feel more and more affinity with the poem "When I Am Old, I Shall Wear Purple"—only I'll embellish that purple fabric with slashing and fraying, bleaching and beading, ribbons and rosettes. When I am old, with Linda's help, I shall never stop embellishing.

Robbie Fanning
StarWear Series Editor

Introduction

Some of us like the extraordinary. We tire easily of the same old thing, the run-of-the-mill, the blasé. We are a special breed of rebels who make our statement, not wildly shouting in the streets, but quietly, at home, in cloth. Give us a bag of iridescent beads, spools of silk thread, and a stack of elegant fabrics, and we will create a masterpiece.

Embellishments is a book for artists in cloth. Whether you make beautiful quilts or exquisite clothing, you'll find fabric manipulations and surface applications to add even more excitement to your designs. I will share time-saving techniques for classic procedures like pleating, tucking, and fringing. I've even unearthed some interesting ethnic embellishment techniques like Native American thongwork. Victoriana lovers will relish the antique ribbonwork ideas.

Even if you don't sew, due to either lack of time or lack of interest, I've added some fabulous ideas you can use to add appeal to your ready-to-wear garments. Add tucked pockets to an overshirt, bead the collar of a silk blouse, stitch new closures to an old love-to-wear blazer, sew rosettes to the brim of a baseball cap, add a patchwork yoke to a shirt, sew fringe to the cowl of a tunic, attach shirred lace panels to the front of a silk blouse, collage a pair of slippers . . . the possibilities are limitless.

I've tried to keep all of the instructions brief and easy to follow to encourage you to try everything. If you discover a technique that is particularly interesting to you, make it a part of your repertoire.

I hope you will use this book as a jumping-off point and take your creations beyond what I've shown you here—break through the barriers and make it sublime!

L.F.K.

[Dress] is one of the most powerful mediums of expression ever devised by humans. It serves as a frontier to the human body and a determinant of the individual's inner consciousness.

—Penny Storm, *Functions of Dress*

The Preliminaries

1

Clothing That Flatters

Well-dressed people have a secret. It's not merely the expense of their clothing, it's the cut and drape of the cloth. By selecting the correct cut and drape for your figure type, you can create the illusion of a proportional figure. Along with color (which I'll discuss later in this chapter), correcting the proportion is one of the major components to looking great. You wear the clothes; they don't wear you.

During the '50s the Marilyn Monroe/Jane Russell hourglass figure was popular, and everyone tried to emulate that look. With the '60s came the flat-chested, slim-hipped Twiggy look, which was difficult for anyone over 22 to copy. Yet the look included the A-line, which cleverly disguised those womanly hips and made the style available to most women. Remember the '70s hemlines? First the mini, then the midi, then the maxi. Oh yes, and the discowear: large, pointed-collared shirts with huge lapels and bell-bottom pants! The '80s found women climbing the corporate ladder in severely styled suits. A floppy neck bow was de rigueur.

Today we've learned that it is okay to show off our feminine side with nice detailing like cutwork collars, pleats, and softly draped suits. We are now entering a new phase in which self-expression is in vogue.

Shapely breasts, a noticeable waist, and slim hips—somewhat like a slender Marilyn Monroe—make the fashionable look for today.

Discovering Your Body Type

Let's take a look at the five basic body types. I'll show you how you can use magical tricks of illusion to create an eye-pleasing figure. The trick is to enhance and camouflage!

Figure 1.1 shows the shape of today's ideal woman. Trace this shape onto onionskin paper. You can use your tracing as an overlay for the five figure shapes to see what needs to be corrected. The five shapes are the triangle, rectangle, circle, heart, and figure-eight (Figure 1.2).

The triangle represents the small-breasted woman with wide hips (Figure 1.3a). If you take your tracing of the perfect figure and lay it over the triangle figure, you can see where the proportion needs to be corrected. Delineate the top half of the body by adding shoulder pads, which bring out the shoulders and balance the hips. Play up the skinny waistline by accenting it with flashy belts. Keep the design interest on the top half of the body.

The rectangular woman has an athletic-style body; it's straight up and down (Figure 1.3b). The idea here is to create the illusion of a waist. One simple trick is to wear a blazer over a sheath dress. Now take a belt and put it on over the dress. You now have a waist; no one can tell how wide your waist is because of the blazer. This camouflage technique works equally well with belted pants and an overshirt.

Circle-shaped women have large breasts, a thick waist, and larger hips (Figure 1.3c). Enhance the shoulders and face. If your legs are nicely proportioned, show them off as often as possible.

The heart-shaped woman has large breasts, a slim waist and slender hips (Figure 1.3d). This is the perfect figure for wearing leggings (show your bottom half off!) with oversize T-shirts and overblouses. If your tummy isn't a problem, tuck

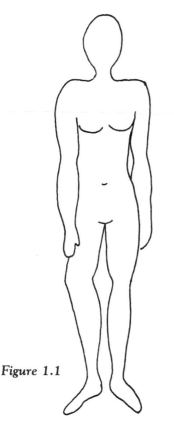

Figure 1.1

Figure 1.2

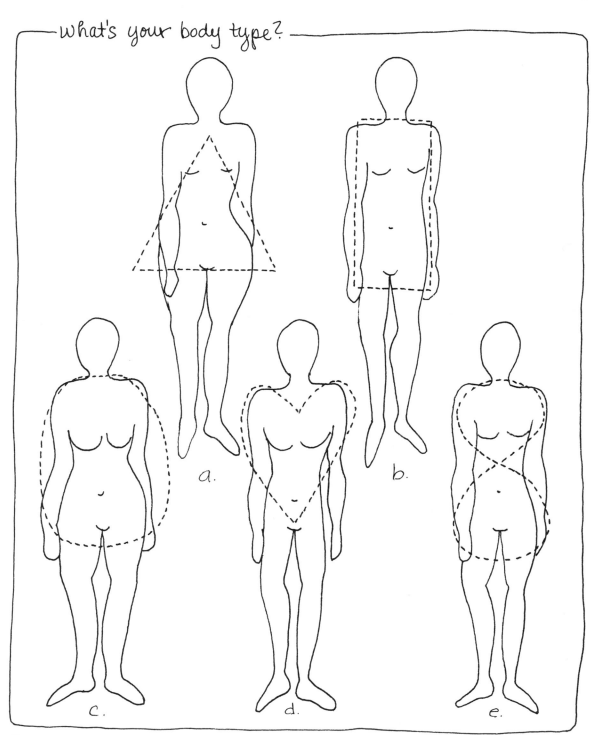

Figure 1.3

in the shirt, throw on a belt, and show off your waist, too. Avoid fluffy details like ruffles and big bows on your shirts. Keep the line smooth and sleek.

All of you ideally shaped women with figure-eight bodies (Figure 1.3e) need little help from my bag of tricks. Thank your parents if it's genetic or thank yourself if you've been working out routinely. You can wear just about anything.

No matter what your figure shape, have fun with clothes. Play up your beauty, and don't wilt away in baggy muumuus. Enjoy everything fashion has to offer.

Selecting the Best Clothing for Your Body Type

As you can see from the experiment you just did with body types, anybody can look very good, regardless of size or shape. Learn to enhance the best parts of your body. Do you know what they are? If not, ask your husband or friends for their opinions. In a recent fashion runway show, Donna Karan displayed pieces with the shoulders cut out and exposed (Figure 1.4). What a smart move! Everybody has good shoulders. Pick out your best parts and intensify their beauty by drawing the eye to that area with bright colors, rhinestones, and glitter. Enhance!

Then there are the parts of your body that you are not very pleased with. Do you have thunder thighs? Jelly upper arms? No waist? Bulgy belly? Don't worry, you can use camouflage and cover up those areas. Try not to make the mistake of wearing really tight clothing over these troublesome areas. That will accentuate rather then detract from the problem. Just as a magician uses misdirection to distract you, you can use fashion to fool the eyes of the beholder. Tone down the problem site and position bright, shiny, attractive elements so they accentuate your best features.

Figure 1.4

Illusionary Tricks

Here's the quintessence of the best tricks of illusion I can share with you. Figures 1.5, 1.6, and 1.7 translate some of this advice into actual outfits.

To look thinner, wear

Smooth clothing, V-neck sweaters; narrow- to medium-width vertical stripes or designs; princess-cut dresses; monotone

Figure 1.5

Figure 1.6

Figure 1.7

outfits (the same color for top and bottom); darker colors in matte finishes.

To look heavier, wear
Oversize, bulky sweaters; lots of texture and design details like large flounces; shiny clothing that attracts a lot of light; chunky shoes in a bright color.

To look taller, wear
Single-breasted jackets; narrow lapels; skinny pants; pointed, princess waistlines; no belts; monotone dressing; smooth, soft textures; taupe shoes.

To look shorter, wear
Portrait collars; full, bouffant sleeves; drindl skirts; large hats; wide belts (in a contrasting color to your outfit); knee-length pants; chunky platform shoes; bold horizontal patterns; bulky textures.

To extend the shoulder line, wear
Shoulder pads; boatneck collars; ruffled, off-the-shoulder peasant blouses; horizontal details; color blocks.

To diminish shoulder width, wear
Sleeveless or halter styles; raglan or dolman sleeves; centered design details or motifs; capes.

To make the face look larger, wear
Boy-cut hair; bold makeup; accents near face; Cleopatra necklaces.

To make the face look smaller, wear
Big hairstyles; no cosmetics; smooth, collarless shirts and jackets; no earrings.

To lengthen the neck (which gives a more regal air to your stature), wear
Short hairstyles (either cut short above the ear or long upswept hair); V-necks; surplice bodices; long pendants; vertical, centered details on clothing.

To shorten a too-thin neck, wear
Strong horizontal lines on clothing; cowls; mandarin or ruffled necklines; long hair; chokers.

To make the bust look fuller, wear
Ruffles; pleats; lace or smocking on the bodice; butterfly or flouncy short sleeves; textured or fuzzy sweaters; straight, skinny skirts.

To camouflage a large bust, wear
Smooth, vertical, patterned bodices; cowl collars; dark, matte colors; full skirts.

To make the waist appear slimmer, wear
Shoulder pads; bright, jazzy motifs near the face; blazers and overshirts belted over pants or skirts; princess waistlines; dark colors at waistline.

To conceal a protruding belly, wear
Overblouses; unconstructed jackets; softly gathered or pleated pants; A-line skirts; gored skirts.

To hide thunder thighs, wear
Long jackets; coatdresses; sweater jackets; softly gathered skirts; dark-colored bottom pieces (bright, sparkly designs can be worn near the face to create diversion).

To make upper arms look thinner, wear
Raglan or dolman sleeves; three-quarter or long sleeves; bright jewelry at wrist and on fingers.

To lengthen a short waist, wear
Long skirts; empire waists; jackets and overblouses; no belt or other design details at the waist; vertical motifs or stripes on bodice.

To shorten a long waist, wear
Wide belts; dropped waists; diagonal details or patterns on the top half of your body.

To make the bottom look smaller, wear
Accents at face and neck; A-line or gored skirts; long jackets that do not stop at the widest part of your body; dark-colored skirts and pants.

To make a flat bottom look curvier, wear
Peplums; full skirts; pegged skirts; dropped waists; nipped-in waists.

To make legs look thinner and longer, wear
Long pants and skirts; hosiery to match your clothing or in darker tones; shoes to match skin tone or hosiery; darker colors on bottom half of your body.

To make legs seem larger and thicker, wear
Short, tight skirts; capri pants; cuffs; chunky shoes; bright, shiny leggings; ribbed or textured hosiery.

To make the feet look smaller, wear
Plain shoes; footwear in colors close to skin tone; medium to small heels; tapered toes.

To make small feet look larger, wear
Two-toned shoes; bright-colored or patent leather footwear; square toes; chunky styles; large, decorative accents like shoe buckles and bows.

Choosing a Style

Once you can see which areas to enhance and which to camouflage, you need to select the style that fits you best. I've defined five different style categories: youthful, sophisticated, casual/sporty, artistic, and feminine/romantic. When you read the description of each category, you may find that you are a combination of styles; many of us are. That's just fine. Be who you want to be. The five categories are merely meant to give you ideas about how to achieve the style you want.

To create the impression of **youthfulness,** wear jumpers, full skirts, bows, and bright, hot colors. Try the following colors: brilliant orange, chartreuse, glowing yellow, and any of the fluorescents, such as acid blue, bright green, and passion purple.

A **sophisticated** look can be achieved by wearing tailored suits, conservative hem lengths, straight skirts, collarless silk shells, solid fabrics or small-scale prints in classic colors. Black, white, taupe, deep wine, and emerald green are some sophisticated colors.

If you prefer a **casual/sporty** look, throw on a sweater without any loud design details (plain or perhaps with a nautical motif is ideal), a man's-style long-sleeved shirt, well-fitting jeans or gabardine pants, and sneakers or loafers. Limit the colors to those found in the earth palette such as khaki, ocean blue, shell pink, ecru, and soft white.

Are you the **artistic** type? Then you like to be noticed and prefer brightly colored, large patterns in both huge florals and wild geometrics. Select clothing without darts or any fussy details; keep the lines smooth and flat. Unconstructed shapes like the Japanese kimono or hipari are ideal canvases for hand-painted designs and outré appliqués. Try lamés in the deep, color-soaked hues of the rainbow, and combine chromas that aren't usually put together. Juxtapose textures, fabric finishes, and design motifs. For example, wear a satin jacket; white pebble-textured sweater; skinny, well-worn jeans that have taken on the patina of age; and bright red patent leather spike heels. Wear hand-crafted jewelry that is loud and bold.

On the other hand, if you are soft and demure, you are the **feminine/romantic** type. The delicate, curvy elements are appropriate for you: laces, gathers, soft pleats, and flounces that are delicate in scale and color are perfect. Jewelry and accessories in the art nouveau motifs of flowers and angels made of gold with a string of pearls add the right final touch.

Accessories

Oh, "accessories" is one of my favorite words in the realm of wearables! Accessories can give a ho-hum outfit real pizzazz. Usually I buy accessories *first*, then create an outfit to coordinate. This approach produces a very professional-looking designer outfit.

I'm always on the lookout for interesting pieces. I've found belts made of exotic leathers; buckles made of brass (amorphous in shape, embedded with stones); kicky see-through plastic belts studded with rhinestones; and a wide, bright-red stretchy belt that is very forgiving of that piece of "must have" chocolate chip cheesecake.

Sashes

Sashes are fun. Here's an easy technique I use to create a plethora of sashes in many colors (Figure 1.8).

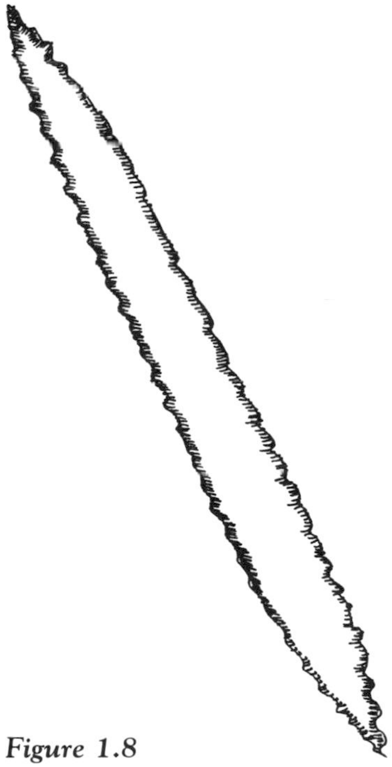

Figure 1.8

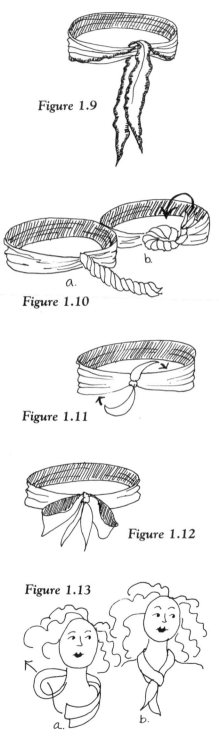

Figure 1.9

Figure 1.10

Figure 1.11

Figure 1.12

QUICK-AND-EASY SASH

1. Cut a piece of stretchy knit 15" wide × 60"–70" long. Taper the ends to a point.
2. Set your serger or sewing machine to make a seam-finishing stitch. Choose thread to match the fabric.
3. Sew around the edges of the scarf, pulling slightly on the cloth to create a ruffled edge.
4. Trim the hanging threads.

That's it. It is so simple, you can make up a batch of these to match your ensembles. Try wearing sashes in a variety of ways. Wrap the sash around your waist twice (three times if you are very skinny), and tie it in a soft knot (down the front or to the side), allowing the ends to dangle (Figure 1.9). Tie the ends of the sash in a rosette (Figure 1.10), simply tie a knot and tuck the ends in under the sash (Figure 1.11), or tie the sash in a soft bow (Figure 1.12). Try using the sashes over sheath dresses or oversized T-shirts—they look great!

If you make the sashes in a shorter length (30" is good), you can tie them around your neck or in your hair. Tie the sash into a loop (Figure 1.13), for example, or wind it around your hair and knot it on top or underneath (Figure 1.14). You could also wrap it around your head and tie it in a sassy bow (Figure 1.15). "A Mini-Course on Color" later in this chapter includes a section on "scarf artistry," which describes more tying ideas.

Figure 1.13

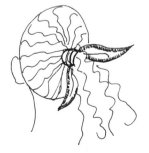

Figure 1.14   **Figure 1.15**

Hats

For a fun outing with a friend, make a date to go hat shopping. Spend an afternoon trying on different hats. You'll giggle a lot, but this is the best way to find the style of hat that makes you look gorgeous. There is a hat shape for everyone. Just keep trying them on until you find one you like. In addition, you can follow these basic guidelines.

If your face is oval, try a portrait-style hat to create a strong horizontal line (Figure 1.16). For a square-shaped face, try a hat with a rounded shape (Figure 1.17), and for a round face, try a beret or a hat cocked on a sharp diagonal (Figure 1.18).

With a stash of a few hats—possibly a straw picture hat, a baseball-style cap, and a wool cloche—you can create many moods (Figure 1.19). Decorate the hats in your style. Add a bunch of silk flowers or some fancy or funky pins (how about all of those quilting guild pins you've been collecting?). Wrap one with a silk scarf or one of the sashes you've just made. I have a pewter pin that holds fresh flowers. I wear it on my hat instead of on my lapel. Each summer morning I fill it full of fresh flowers from my garden.

OVAL FACE

Figure 1.16

SQUARE FACE

Figure 1.17

ROUND FACE

Figure 1.18

STRAW HAT

Figure 1.19

BASEBALL HAT

CLOCHE

Footwear

Everyone needs at least one pair of classic pumps. Try black or taupe (a color that makes you look taller and your feet look smaller—it's one of the classic neutrals). Flats look great with long skirts. Summer beckons for a pair of brightly colored espadrilles and a kicky little shoe in pure white. Of course, sneakers are mandatory for any serious exercise program or a day of mall shopping. Short cowgirl boots are great looking with short flirt skirts. And those of us that live in the north tundra must have a pair of practical, warm, waterproof boots.

Jewelry

Here's the dazzler! Use the precious metals to bring out and enhance the colors in your clothing. Gold sparkles on black, white, royal to navy blue, and dark chocolate browns. Silver looks terrific with pinks, blues (pale to navy), black, and white. If the garment you are wearing has lamé or other metallic accents, use the same color jewelry. The newest hot idea is to use white (silver, white gold, or platinum) and yellow metals together. There's even rose- and green-gold. This multihued jewelry goes with almost anything. No guesswork.

If you are a fan of artists' jewelry, you can explore all of the possibilities—handwoven, wrapped, beaded, ceramic, porcelain, Fimo clay, and so on. I have an array of interesting pins, mostly handmade by myself or other jewelry artisans. I wear a golden winged goddess when I have a large project to tackle; a silver cloisonné Screaming Mimi pin is reserved for times I want to shout from the rooftops. I also have a huge collection of costume jewelry from the '40s and '50s that belonged to my mother. I like to wear these pieces to family reunions.

I love jewelry. I wear at least one fresh piece everyday, along with my "never-take-it-off" stuff, like my wedding rings and a special bracelet.

If you prefer costume jewelry, make no apologies. We can treasure it all. Jewelry makes a loud statement as to who you are and how you see yourself. One dazzling piece can set the stage for the drama you play out in your clothes.

¡AY CARAMBA! PINS

I've made many of these special ¡Ay Caramba! pins. They are very simple to fashion but look complicated and interesting. Try one or two or three.

MATERIALS

Campaign-type buttons with pin on back

Small snippets of cloth, ribbon, thread (leftovers from the "Confetti Mosaics" in Chapter 3, Manipulations, can be used), paper pieces, and memorabilia (stamps, stickers, tickets, etc.)

Beads

Metal charms

Gloss polymer medium (available at art- and crafts-supply stores)

PROCEDURE

1. Generously coat the face of the button with polymer medium. Immediately start to imbed the snippets and fragments in the medium. The larger, flat pieces should go on first. This will form the background and cover up any writing on the button.
2. Using more medium, add all of the other three-dimensional objects you wish to incorporate on your pin (Figure 1.20). Try sprinkling it with beads. Let the pin dry
3. Coat the face of the pin generously with more polymer medium—all paper and cloth items should be saturated with medium. Let it dry again.

Figure 1.20

Once you've tried this technique, you can start collecting items to incorporate in your next batch of pins. How about doing theme pins? One in watch parts; another with cherubs. Or possibly do a pin to commemorate an important event or outing—a wedding, a special play, the birth of a new baby.

Put it all together: body type, style, accessories, and the tricks of illusion. Now you have a good idea of what will enhance your charms and camouflage your figure flaws. Use this as a key to picking out sewing patterns and ready-to-wear clothing.

Calico, chintz, gingham, madras, and muslin all originated in India.

UNCONSTRUCTED JACKET

CONSTRUCTED JACKET

Figure 1.21

Sewing Your Own Style

I would like to share my concept of sewing with you. I sew primarily to create one-of-a-kind outfits. If there is a garment already available on the market, I'll buy it. I don't waste my time trying to create an outfit someone has already perfected in design and workmanship. I will purchase a nicely tailored blazer that shouts, "I'm a canvas—take me home and embellish me." The structure of the garment is already there. Although some artists purchase prestretched canvas, other artists buy canvas and stretch it themselves. The choice is yours: It really depends on what part of clothing-making is most interesting to you.

Do you enjoy tailoring? Then buy cloth and do it. If the part of embellished clothing that intrigues you is the applied decoration, buy a finished garment and go from there. No one says you have to create a garment from scratch.

My own way of going about it is as follows. Unconstructed garments (Figure 1.21)—those with no darts and few pattern pieces, like pullover shirts, simple jackets, and two-piece skirts—I make from scratch. I'm involved in the total process from the inception of the idea to fabric and thread selection to the final finished garment.

When I want nicely tailored clothing, I purchase it and then embellish it in my studio. It's the best of both worlds.

Pattern Selection

I rarely buy commercial patterns anymore. There are a number of reasons. First, they have too many pattern pieces. Second, too many adjustments need to be made for a correct fit. Finally, cutting out the cloth is not one of my passions. I can hear you saying, "Okay, then how do you do it?"

Well, I've found the best patterns by copying ready-to-wear. That's my secret. It's that simple, and I bet once you've tried this method, you will use it too. Ready-to-wear offers many speedy sewing tips, too. You just need to investigate the garment: Look closely at the order of construction, the way the seams are finished, and other details.

Here are some basic guidelines for working with ready-to-wear: The garment you wish to copy must be unconstructed, and the garment should have only a few pattern pieces. Let me give you a concrete example so you can visualize along with me.

HOW TO MAKE A DESIGNER SHIRT "EZ-TRACE" PATTERN

For this process you'll need a favorite sweatshirt and some nonwoven, nonfusible interfacing.

1. Take a simple sweatshirt from your dresser. Don't select one with raglan sleeves—that's more difficult to copy (Figure 1.22). You want one with a dropped-shoulder sleeve. Pick the shirt that fits you best, the one that makes you feel good every time you put it on. Don't worry . . . we won't demolish your perfect-fitting sweatshirt. It won't be taken apart at all.

2. Fit is one of the main reasons I sew by this method. If I own a piece of clothing that fits very well, I want to have more pieces like that hanging in my closet.

3. To trace the pattern, you will need nonwoven, nonfusible interfacing (Do-sew and Trace-A-Pattern are two brand names). You can get by using tissue paper or newspaper (at least one week old, so it won't bleed ink; some people use doctor's examining paper), but the interfacing will give you a truer pattern because it won't shift as much as the paper does. This will be your master pattern, and you'll use it many, many times. Hypothetically, you could create a million different shirts from this one pattern.

4. If you analyze the components of the sweatshirt, you'll see three pieces—a front, a back, and a sleeve (Figure 1.23). These are the pieces you will be tracing.

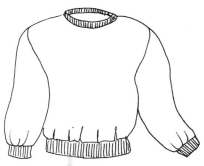

dropped-shoulder
sleeve

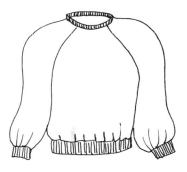

RAGLAN
SLEEVE

Figure 1.22

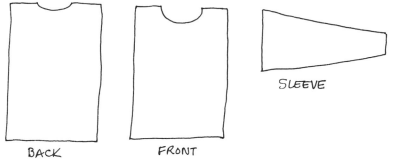

SLEEVE

BACK   FRONT

Figure 1.23

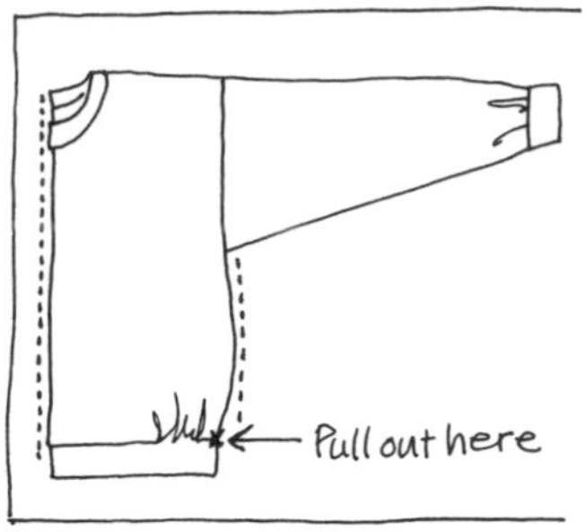

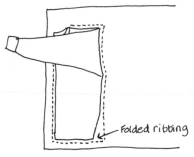

Figure 1.24

Figure 1.25

5. Lay a length of interfacing on a table. Fold the sweatshirt in half lengthwise and place it on the interfacing (Figure 1.24). Flatten out the fabric so you don't have any wrinkles. Following Figure 1.24, draw a line on the interfacing along the front of the sweatshirt. Mark where the bottom ribbing begins. Now trace along the side of the sweatshirt, starting at the armpit and stopping at the bottom ribbing of the sweatshirt (see Figure 1.24). To create the straight bottom edge of the pattern, be sure to stretch out the bottom of the shirt to get a true pattern. Don't overstretch; just pull it out to where it would lie if it weren't gathered to the ribbing. Fold the ribbing under the shirt and trace along the bottom edge (Figure 1.25). Don't add any seam allowances at this time.

6. Fold the sleeve to the front of the shirt to get it out of your way. Draw the sleeve seam curve on your pattern (see Figure 1.25). Place the sleeve so it's flat again. Next, draw the shoulder line and then the back neck line (Figure 1.26). Discount the neck ribbing by folding it back out of your way. Mark the front neck line on your pattern, pushing the ribbing out of your way.

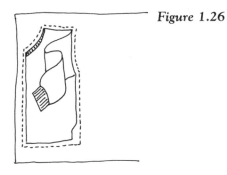

Figure 1.26

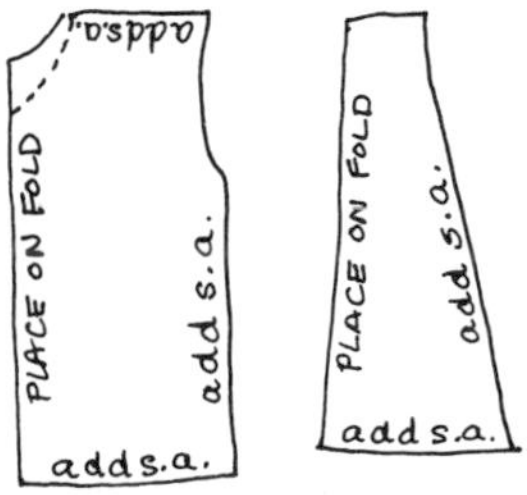

7. Remove the shirt and mark your pattern. Write "place on fold" down the front and "add seam allowance" on the other edges of the pattern (Figure 1.27). Cut out the pattern, adding the seam allowance as you cut. If you feel more comfortable using a pattern with a seam allowance already gauged, add the seam allowances before you cut out the pattern.

8. Make the pattern for the sleeve using the same technique as noted in Steps #5 to #7.

Figure 1.27

9. Measure the ribbing on the existing shirt and use it to buy ribbing in the same width and length to make your own shirts. There may be times when you wish to use no ribbing on the bottom edge (Figure 1.28). Either cut as is from your pattern if you want a short top or add 4″ to 5″ to the length of the pattern before cutting for a longer top. Actually, you can cut it as long as you like, although you may have to add side slits to a long tunic so the garment will fit over your hips (Figure 1.29).

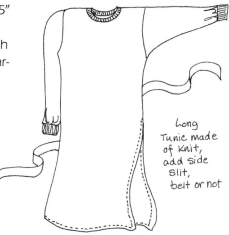

Long Tunic made of Knit, add side slit, belt or not

Figure 1.29

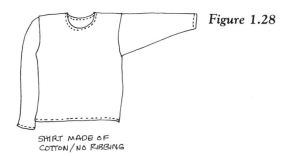

Figure 1.28

SHIRT MADE OF COTTON / NO RIBBING

The beauty of this pattern is that you know it will fit before you even start to create the garment. This process of pattern making may sound difficult, but believe me, it takes longer to explain it than to do it. And you only have to do it once (remember the hypothetical million shirts?).

The resulting pattern can be used with all sorts of cloth—sweatshirt fleece, knits, and even cottons. The over-sized, untailored fit works well with just about any fabric.

Adapting the pattern is easy. For example, cut it open down the front, add seam binding and a zipper, and you have a baseball-style jacket (Figure 1.30). Add buttonholes and jazzy buttons, handmade closures (Figure 1.31), or just leave

BASEBALL-STYLE JACKET

Figure 1.30

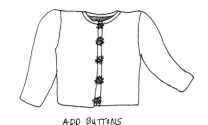

ADD BUTTONS

Figure 1.31

CHANEL-STYLE
OPEN FRONT JACKET

Figure 1.32

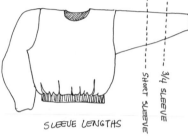

SLEEVE LENGTHS

Figure 1.33

The first doily was a
linen napkin given to
Queen Anne of England
(ruled 1702–1714) by a
man named Doyley.

it open (Figure 1.32). It's your choice, and each modification
will change the look the final garment evokes.

Want a different sleeve? Make up the garment, then before adding the sleeves, try it on. Mark and cut the sleeves to
three-quarter length, short sleeves, or whatever length you
prefer (Figure 1.33). Add ribbing or not.

The pattern can become whatever you desire.

You can use this "EZ-Trace" method to copy many of
the clothing pieces you may already own. Try it on simple
jumpers, straight skirts, plain drop-waist dresses, and T-tops.
It works for leggings and unconstructed jackets, too. I love
jackets and make lots of them.

If you prefer to use commercial patterns, go ahead and
use them—just look for the same components as you would
in an "EZ-Trace" garment: unconstructed with few pattern
pieces. If you have more time than I do and tailoring is your
forte, stay with what you do best. I love extremely tailored
clothes, too. It's just that I want to make more than one or
two garments a year. When you concentrate on the features
of sewing that you value, the experience will be more enjoy-
able.

No-Guilt Sewing

A fabric store that I frequent is billed as one of the best
sewing stores in America. They carry some of the most exquisite cloth: fine meltons, drapey challises, rattlesnake skin,
and hand-painted cloth from Africa. Beautiful! Just to walk
around and feel and see the cloth is an experience.

At the weekly show-and-tell, the demonstrators pass
around a sample garment showing uses for a new product or
perhaps a time-saving sewing technique. The demonstrators
often admonish, "Don't look at the seams" or "I didn't get
the casing sewn closed, so don't look there."

When I first started going to the meetings, I was
shocked at how unfinished the garments were. And the demonstrators were going to wear these outfits to parties the same
evening! I thought *everything* had to be completely finished
before you could wear it. This revelation freed me from that
rigid thought pattern. Now if I don't have a garment finished
in time for an important event . . . so what? I wear it anyway. I don't mean to advocate that you go out with threads

hanging from your hem or a sleeve hanging off. No, I'm just talking about the inside details that can be finished later.

I share this story with you so you realize not to take sewing (even art-to-wear) so seriously. Have fun and create wonderful garments. That's what it's all about. Don't be afraid to break a rule if it will save you time and accomplish the same result.

Just how many times will you actually wear that garment? Once or twice? When we sew, we aren't building a house we expect to last a hundred years. We are expressing who we are at the moment.

When I look at my wardrobe, I find very few pieces older than five years that I even wear anymore. Styles and your shape change over time. Of course, the classics, like my cashmere coat, are good forever. If you make or buy thousand-dollar gowns, naturally you'll want to preserve them for a long time. But most clothing is actually worn for a short period of time.

Those of us who are artists in cloth are willing to speak out with our clothing. We are willing to express who we are today.

Before 1900 all children wore dresses.

Men's suit coats still hold remnants of the past. The buttons on the cuffs, although purely decorative today, were once used to keep long-flowing shirt cuffs out of the way while the men worked and fought. The slit at the back originally functioned to spread the coat when the man rode a horse.

A Mini-Course on Color

The concept and application of color is an important part of design. In this section we'll take a look at the ways color can be used to your advantage.

Figure 1.34 shows a color wheel. If you have colored pencils on hand, go ahead and color in the circles. This will give you a better understanding of exactly how the color wheel is used as we go through the guidelines.

Red, yellow, and blue are called the primaries. They are basic, pure, and naive. All colors are made from these three. The secondary colors—green, violet, and orange—are combinations of the primaries. Green is a mixture of yellow and blue, violet is a red and blue mix, and orange is a combination of red and yellow. To understand this principle more fully, I suggest you try it for yourself. Buy only three jars of paint—one each of the primaries—and mix them in equal portions. Then you will see the magic firsthand.

Now to take color theory even further, try to mix the

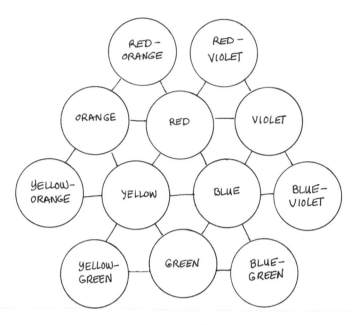

COLOR WHEEL FOR COLOR MIXING

Figure 1.34

tertiaries. These colors are mixtures of a primary and a secondary color. By their names alone you will be able to see the obvious combinations. Red-violet is a combination of red (primary color) and violet (secondary color). Yellow-green is the fusion of yellow and green. The other tertiaries on the color wheel are blue-violet, blue-green, red-orange, and yellow-orange. You may be more familiar with their colloquial names: purple, turquoise, fuchsia, chartreuse, coral, and tangerine. The paint companies try to give exciting one-word names to the colors.

The next interesting color trick is to use the addition of white to the individual colors to make tints and to use the addition of black to make shades (Figure 1.35). A dollop of white added to red makes pink. Note that white can be added in more generous proportions than black; add black a drop at a time.

Brown is created by mixing together red, yellow, and a small amount of blue. Black is the absence of all color and absorbs light. White is a mix of all colors and reflects light. Gray is white mixed with a dash of black.

			PURE COLOR			
←—— TINTS ——→				←—— SHADES ——→		
LIGHTEST BLUE	LIGHTER BLUE	LIGHT BLUE	BLUE	DARK BLUE	DARKER BLUE	DARKEST BLUE

Figure 1.35

Another way to create colors in a more sophisticated range is to add a bit of the complementary color (Figure 1.36). These combinations are found directly across the color wheel. For example, the complement of red is green, the complement of yellow is violet, and the complement of blue is orange.

Speaking of the complementary colors brings us to accepted color schemes. The complements, just discussed, are often used to grab attention. When these colors are used in equal intensities and placed next to one another, they create an undulating effect. In its place, this intriguing color reac-

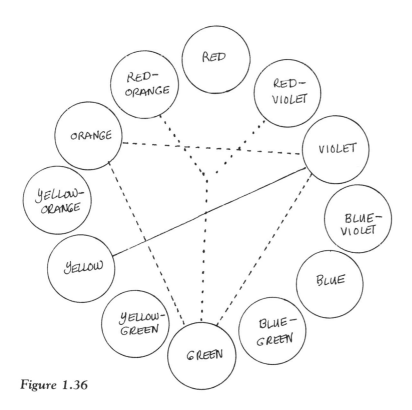

Figure 1.36

The generic term for nylon came from the idea that the newly invented "Fiber 66" would be ideal for no-run hosiery. But the fiber did run, so manufacturers spelled it backward, "nuron," from which evolved the word "nylon."

tion can be used to your benefit. If you don't want the wavy effect, but want to use the complements together, just modify the intensity. Try toning down one or both of the colors.

A monochromatic color scheme is made of one single color. Three blues—pale blue, medium blue, and navy—create a monochromatic color scheme. Any two or more shades and tints of one color used together make up a monochromatic color scheme. This concept is one of the easiest to grasp for people just learning about the principles of color and is often employed. How many times have you grabbed a tan blouse to wear with your chocolate-brown suede skirt?

Colors have a warm or cool feeling. If you were painting a dragonfly and wanted it to look like a hot, steamy afternoon, you would use reds, yellows, and oranges. For a cool effect, you would use blues, greens, and violets.

Colors also have weight. A dark blue suit gives the impression of more weight than a light blue suit. Use this fact to control your environment. In the summer, wear the light blue suit to look vivacious and buoyant. You'll look cooler. In winter wear bright, warm-colored sweaters in reds, yellows, and oranges. You'll feel warmer without turning up the thermostat.

Texture also adds weight and warmth. A smooth, finely woven cotton will look much lighter than a nubby bouclé knit.

The Symbolism of Color

Red
Hot, very active, and alive. Associated with fire, blood, danger, and passion. Signifies emergency, wakefulness, lack of time, and hunger. Often used in restaurants because it activates the salivary gland.

Orange
Hot, eccentric, and naive. A very stimulating color. The color of sunset in the tropics, fruits, and flowers. Not used much in its pure form in clothing (is usually tinted to tone it down). Not an easy color to wear. Try as an accessory. Symbolizes enjoyment of the unusual.

Yellow
Warm and festive. The color of the sun. Associated with expectancy, youthfulness, and joy. An active color. Can be juvenile in its pure form. Symbolizes spontaneity and smiles.

Green

Cool and the symbol of nature. Associated with environmental awareness, jealousy, and money. Eases tension. Denotes hope.

Blue

Very cool and serene. Restful. The color of water and the sky. Signifies fidelity and fairness.

Violet

Cool. Associated with frivolity, royalty, vanity, and pride. The color of cottage garden flowers, eggplant, and amethyst. Connotes boldness, comfortableness, and nonconformity.

White

Neutral. The symbol of purity, simplicity, and innocence. One of the most stunning colors. Signifies virtue and illumination.

Black

Neutral. The most dramatic color. Signifies mystery, death, elegance, and seriousness. Denotes persistence, determination, and haughtiness.

Colors to Enhance the Real You

A number of color programs have been available in the past few years. Most of these plans employ a color palette based on the four seasons: spring, summer, autumn, and winter. Each "season" can wear a full range of colors; what changes is the shade or tone of the color. While a "spring" can wear a pale pink, a "summer" looks more appealing in a deep, clear pink. "Autumn" enjoys the oranges, taupes, and khaki, while "winter" can carry off the clear, bold colors.

If you haven't had your colors "done," you can still use a number of tricks to make the application of color less of a mystery. The right color appears to erase years from your age and makes you look well rested and vital. Have you noticed how certain garments always get compliments every time you wear them? These garments—their styles and colors—offer great clues to what is right for you.

To find out what colors are best for you, hold pieces of clothing up to your face in front of a mirror. You'll be able to see the difference right away. If you have trouble distinguishing between the colors, invite a friend over to help you see the disparity. Some colors will truly spark up your face.

Early liberationist Amelia Bloomer was one of the first to introduce pants to women. "Bloomers" were not accepted until World War II, when women replaced men in the factories. Flowing, billowy clothing caught in the machinery too easily. This is the principal reason for the very tailored look of the '40s. Even actress Veronica Lake bobbed her peek-a-boo hair at the request of the government. Long hair was too dangerous in the workplace.

As you age, your hair and skin color begin to fade (unless you are very lucky). The more narrow the range between hair and skin color the less color choices available to make you look attractive. At this point in your life you'll need to make a decision to go either with the bright, clear colors or the very soft pastels. Either will enhance your magnificence. Stay away from the muddied, midtone colors.

Scarf Artistry

You can wear any color as long as you wear one of your "good" colors next to your face. If black isn't a good color (does it make you look pale and sallow?), you can still wear that black sheath as long as you drape a scarf over your shoulder in one of the colors that puts light in your face.

Every woman should own a bevy of scarves. Buy them or better yet make your own using some of the techniques in this book. Stenciling, stamping, and hand painting are all possibilities. Then add a fringe or some beading. A good selection of scarves can double or triple your wardrobe alternatives.

If you want to try making your own scarves, here are a range of possible sizes. A handkerchief size is a 6″ or 10″ square. The shoulder scarf runs between a 32″ and 36″ square. A short (tuck-in) neck scarf is approximately 10″ × 20″. One of my favorites is the long neck scarf, 18″ × 72″. This one can be worn around the neck as well as at the waist or hip as a belt or sash.

In addition to simply tying a scarf loosely around your neck or throwing it over your shoulder, you can attempt the innovative scarf drapes illustrated in Figure 1.37.

Figure 1.37

LONG SQUARE
KNOT

GLORIA COWL

TRIANGLE DRAPE

SIDE SWING

FLOPPY BOW

Universal Colors

Certain colors have the ability to bring out the best in nearly everyone. I call these colors the universals—royal blue, coral, and purple. Use these colors as your secret arsenal. If you can't decide what to wear, dress in these colors and you will look and feel good all day. Buy or make lots of accessories in these colors to pep up outfits that have a tendency to drain the color from your face.

Classic-colored clothing is always a good investment. Black and navy blue are "must haves," especially in the winter season. White is right too. I prefer a clear, pure white. For your skin tone you may prefer a champagne, soft white, or ecru.

The Affinity of Color

One of the most intriguing concepts concerning the use of color came to me from a favorite art and philosophy teacher who summered in Paris, spent early autumn in the Orient, and endured her winters in the Midwest. She had studied with some of the best painters. Where on her travels she unearthed this gem I'll never know, but I appreciate the beauty of the concept, and I know it works wonders.

Instead of looking at a color as a single entity, she rationalized that a color should be regarded in terms of its relationship to other colors. In other words, how a color looks, reflects, and reacts to the other color or colors lying next to it is of primary importance. The relationship, or affinity, is based on a Bright-Light-Dark (B-L-D) concept.

A simple example of B-L-D affinity would be **Bright (B) = yellow, Light (L) = white, and Dark (D) = brown.** This is only one sample of an infinite variety of color combinations.

To better understand the B-L-D concept of color, follow medium blue through the following chart.

Sample Bright-Light-Dark (B-L-D) Progressions

Bright	Light	Dark
Medium blue	Pale yellow	Brick red
Orange	Medium blue	Chocolate brown
Chartreuse	Ecru	Medium blue

The chart shows how a color can move within the B-L-D progression to become bright, light, or dark, depending on the three colors chosen.

Another important tenet of the affinity color theory is to use the colors in unequal amounts. In a three-part color scheme, select one of the colors to become the main color, used in the largest amount. The second color should be used less frequently. Finally, add the "spark," or the color used to accent and create tension. Using the first color combination in the chart given earlier, I would use mostly brick red, add a good amount of pale yellow fabric, and then spark it with the medium blue.

The B-L-D concept can be expanded to accommodate any number of colors. Here is a color chart used to make a quilt.

B-L-D Color Choices Used by the Author in a Quilt

Bright Colors (used as accent sparks)	Light Colors (used for one-third of the quilt)	Dark Colors (used for two-thirds of the quilt)
Scarlet	Medium blue	Black
Light peach	Medium green	Emerald
Bright yellow		
Electric green		

B-L-D = Bright-Light-Dark

If you were to analyze some of your most promising work, you may find you already employ this theory without consciously recognizing it. Try it; I believe you will be surprised by the results.

The Importance of Design

Once you've mastered the techniques described in this book using predrawn patterns and motifs, you may hunger to create a piece of art-to-wear that is entirely your own.

Train your eye to see art by exposing yourself to the best specimens. Go to art galleries, museums, fine-art fairs—

seek out concrete examples of art. Soon you will begin to see the art in everything, including fish in an aquarium, telephone lines, a pile of rocks, and the way a person moves on a baseball field.

Begin by collecting interesting examples in clips from newspapers, magazines, postcards, photographs, menus, and so on. Collect them in one place and call it your design cache. Always be on the lookout for good design. Carry a small notebook with you and make sketches in it. Don't worry that you can't draw; often it is most important to catch the impression of an idea. A few lines can capture the spirit of the design.

Here's something else to try: Make a simple viewfinder from mat board. Cut two right angle forms about 2″ wide. Using some of the clips from your cache, place the right angles on the design. Move them around, spread them apart, move them closer until you find an interesting section. This is an excellent way to create an abstract design. Tape the viewfinder in place and take the clip to a commercial print shop. Use their copy machine to enlarge the design to the size you wish to reproduce.

Another way to make your own designs is to take a mundane item and do it in repeats. Andy Warhol did this with Campbell soup cans and started a career. Or blow up an everyday item à la Claes Oldenburg; for example, he might take a simple spoon and makes it huge, taking it out of context.

Patterning can create design motifs too. Take a basic motif such as a diamond (Figure 1.38). Try overlapping the motif—a little or a lot (Figure 1.39). You could box the motif to form a larger pattern (Figure 1.40). Now add another

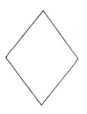

Figure 1.38

Figure 1.39

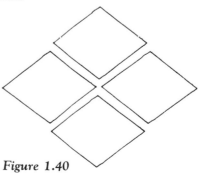

Figure 1.40

design element; for example, try a circle (Figure 1.41). Use one of the motifs as a central core (Figure 1.42). Try stacking the design elements (Figure 1.43). Jumble the motifs to get a pattern with movement (Figure 1.44).

Here are a few more ideas. Because words suggest different visual perceptions for each individual, you will interpret each of these "word sketches" in your own technique and style. (That's why I haven't illustrated them.) Try 'em!

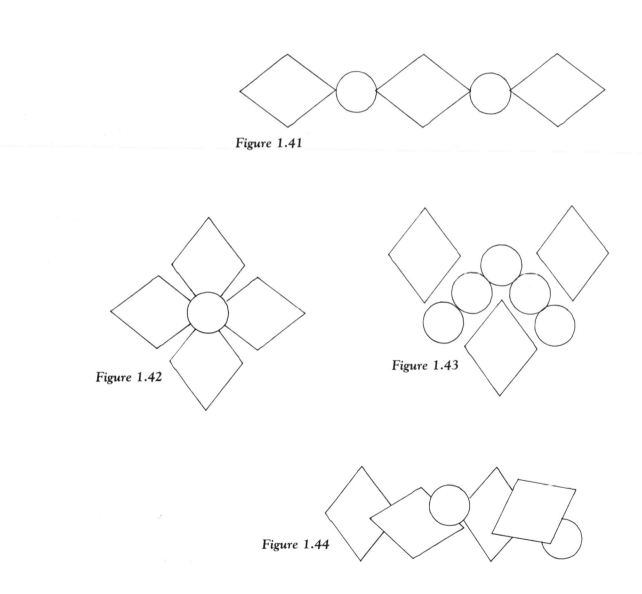

Figure 1.41

Figure 1.42

Figure 1.43

Figure 1.44

DESIGN INSPIRATION

- Enlarge traditional quilt patterns and use only part of the design.
- Use one large design element set at an unusual angle to create a jolt to the eye.
- Play with basic geometric shapes to develop fresh imagery.
- Try rubber-stamping images in a semicircular fan design, use cutouts, or do appliqué. Throw on spatter paint to blend the design into the background.
- Work slices and diagonal chunks of cloth into long strips.
- Change repetitive images by using vibrant color gradations.
- Try unusual imagery—bathroom fixtures or basement pipes, for example.
- Strip piece a pictorial.
- Make a design within a design.
- Stuff some elements for a three-dimensional effect.
- Color block by using large geometric-shaped pieces of colored fabric, then insert black strips.
- Use a different format. If the motif runs vertically, redraw it to fit a horizontal panel.
- Use unconventional cloth—try denim for a party dress detail, for instance.

FRONT

Placing Motifs on Garments

Cloth artists need to take design a step further. Because we are not designing on a flat plane, as in a painting or a quilt, we need to take into consideration the rounded shape of the body and the way it moves. In essence, we are creating a form of kinetic art that will change with the movement of the body and be seen from many different angles.

The first design technique is to accentuate the soft curvy shape of the body and use flowing, rounded motifs. A good example would be a large floral appliqué that runs diagonally across the chest, up to the shoulder. To add a bit of intrigue, continue the design a bit over the shoulder (Figure 1.45). From the back view, the design element becomes a

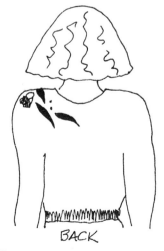

BACK

Figure 1.45

"teaser." Curiosity lures the viewer to the front of the garment.

To fully embrace the rounded human form, bring the design all the way to the back. Just remember to keep the design flowing, with no right angles.

The second method is to use geometric shapes. Look at the current rage of color blocking for an excellent example of this technique (Figure 1.46). If you look and really "see," you will find that the most pleasing examples use the color in uneven amounts, with an asymmetrical placement.

The best way to see if a design is working is to pin the motifs in place on a mannequin and take a look from all angles. Does the design work? If not, move the elements. When the design clicks, you'll know. Be confident and rely on your own judgment.

> "Art is not handicraft, it is the transmission of feeling. . . ."
> —Leo Tolstoy (What Is Art?, 1898)

Figure 1.46

Cloth
Transformations

2

Finding the Right Cloth

There are many wonderful new fabrics to choose from at any well-stocked sewing store. You can find boldly patterned florals, color-soaked cottons, or demure pastels. Everything is at your fingertips, and the staff can be extremely helpful.

Yet there are other ways to add to your collection without buying new cloth. Garage sales, estate sales, and resale shows are on my "A" list. You never know what you may find, and it's always a bargain.

One of my fabric hunts unearthed a 5-yard length of exquisite shantung silk. I've also found stacks of decorator fabric samples. I cut away the motifs—mostly huge, colorful birds and giant, jazzy florals—and appliqué them onto jackets and skirts.

Don't overlook other secondhand goodies, such as tins of old, interesting buttons, that you can pick up for a song. Friends and neighbors are good sources for cloth too. Just be sure the word gets out that you are a fabric artist. Even if they don't sew, they may be ready to discard old clothing. I've received beautiful old silk dresses printed with ferns and geometrics (from the early '40s) and a nice bundle of '30s pastel miniflorals in 100 percent cotton. And when these friends and neighbors tell their friends and neighbors about this person they know that creates wild clothing, the domino effect goes into action. Soon you'll find yourself inundated with bags of cloth from people you don't even know. Often I'll come home to find bundles at my back door. The package not only gives me more interesting cloth to work with, but it also gives me a push to get sewing if I've been in a funk.

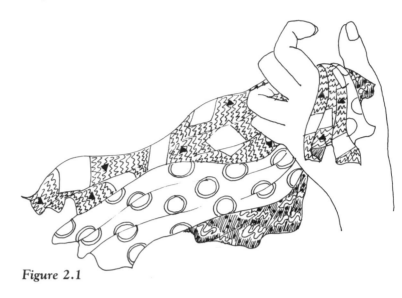

Figure 2.1

Many of the quilting guilds in my area hold annual fabric exchange parties. Each member is asked to bring a 1-yard length of "ugly" cloth to swap for another member's "ugly" cloth. One of the smaller guilds uses a musical chairs approach for redistribution of the cloth. The larger guild, with nearly 400 members, gives each piece of cloth a number, then each participant selects a corresponding number out of a fishbowl.

When I was editor of *Threads & Fibers*, I tried another exchange idea. My husband and I were attending poetry slams at the Green Mill in Chicago—the slams were poetry as performance, very free and inventive. I thought this same concept could translate to cloth art slams—quilts as performance of the imagination—and proposed the idea in *T&F*. A total of 12 readers participated.

Each received a list of materials—1½ yards dark cloth; ¾ yard bright cloth; ¼ yard of two light-colored fabrics; 3 yards of cord, heavy thread, or specialty yarn; 16 large beads; 30 small beads; a spool of thread; and a surprise. The materials were to come from those on hand and all materials were to be used in the project. Once you assembled the supplies from your own sources, you could submit them to *T&F*. If you sent in a box of goodies, you received a box in exchange.

The quilt slam was to encourage working with materials

unfamiliar to the artist and to encourage wild, free abandon of his or her creativity.

The results were extraordinary. Most of the quilts were interesting abstracts, but one quilt I remember vividly was of a vibrant fire-eating dragon made by Carol Boyer of New York.

Try a quilt slam with friends or guild members. It's a great way to recycle materials and spark inventiveness.

Some quilt guilds are using "ugly" cloth for "challenge" quilts in which the sewer incorporates the "ugly" cloth into a small wall quilt of his or her own design.

Fabric outlets are a possibility for interesting cloth, too. Sometimes you need to do some serious searching to locate these well-hidden businesses. They usually are located in industrial parks. One local comforter company has a little store at the back of its warehouse. Here you can get remnants (by remnants they mean pieces of polished cottons up to 4 yards long, and the width runs extra wide, too!) and big bags of polyester stuffing, all for pennies compared with what a retail store would charge. A friend of mine in Indiana buys all of her satins at a casket factory. Check around and find out what's being manufactured in your area. You may be pleasantly surprised. Networking with other sewers can give you many leads. Most will graciously share their sources. Join a group in your town; if one doesn't exist, start one.

Your Fabric Stash

If you've already purchased a plethora of cloth, it's time to fess up about storage. I know of one fabric artist who has filled the rafters of her garage with boxes of fabric: She ran out of room in her house.

I'd like to deal with that abundance of unused cloth you have secreted away in your house. Why haven't you used it? Were you unable to coordinate the lengths of yardage into one outfit? Did the color or fabric motifs go out of style before you had a chance to use it? Or did you simply tire of it?

I must admit in print that I too have hoarded more cloth than I will be able to use in this lifetime.

Last year, when my studio became so chock-full of stuff that I almost couldn't enter the door, I knew the time had come to be ruthless. Oh sure, most of the goodies were neatly stacked in labeled boxes, but I was at the point where I was getting claustrophobic in my own workspace. Anything became a candidate for disposal.

Some things were simple to get rid of—outdated papers, back copies of a sewing journal I once published, and such. I didn't even realize that I had five drafting tables: one table, a deluxe portable, and three simple flat ones in various sizes left over from art workshops some years back. Two of them became presents to artist friends. Most of the other things were given to friends and family busy pursuing their dreams in the fields of art, drafting, woodworking, and illustration. I'm quite sure the items found good homes and will be well used.

Then I came to the cloth. As a graphic artist works with paint as her medium, so an art-to-wear artist uses her collection of cloth. The decision to part with some of it was difficult. Now, a year later, I realize my decision wasn't that bad.

Six large plastic bags of double knits (dropped off a month earlier by a friend cleaning out her sewing room) were given to a local quilting group that does many community projects—one year they made quilts for residents of a senior citizen's home, another year they made quilts for AIDS babies in hospitals. These institutions prefer hard-wearing double knits that can hold up under the harsh treatment they get in huge industrial washers and dryers.

Some of the fabric was donated to the Salvation Army, Goodwill, and a local thrift shop. I felt some other home sewers might like to have some fun finding these treasures at their outlet stores.

By then I was finally down to a manageable stack of cloth. I still had some that I really didn't like. Suddenly the "Aha" struck. . . . I could transform the cloth into something more wonderful, more magical, more usable. This chapter includes many techniques for doing just that.

Painting Ho-Hum Cloth

My first thought was to use fabric paint to transform this ho-hum cloth. Paint can cover anything and make it look better. I tried a spatter-and-drip technique.

Fill a toothbrush with paint. Then run a stick or tongue depressor across the bristles of the toothbrush, directing the paint onto the cloth. (Instead of a toothbrush, you may want to experiment with the new spatter applicator made specifically for this technique. I haven't had a chance to try it, but it is supposed to enable you to direct the paint more easily.)

When I wanted a stronger statement, I filled various bottles, such as old ketchup, cosmetic, and shampoo bottles, with paint and literally squeezed it onto the fabric: thin and linear in some areas, large and blotchy in others. One of the neatest applicators is a plastic syringe available from Dharma Trading Company. It is excellent for skinny, squiggly lines. This was total fun. Try it with any color of fabric paint you have on hand. Be free and bold.

With fabric painting, as with all of the techniques described in this book, I encourage you to experiment and let yourself go. In many cases I've provided a list of hints and options to help spark your imagination. If you experiment on cloth that you wouldn't use in its original state anyway, there's no loss. If you don't like your results, pass the fabric on to a friend. As the old saying goes, "One man's meat is another man's poison." (I recall attending a lecture by a fabric artist in which she discussed her hand-dyed silks. She showed an example of what can happen if you leave the cloth in the steamer too long. The edges of the silk were burned, but I thought the burned-edged piece was beautiful.)

Remember, too, that you don't have to use the cloth whole. You may elect to cut it into smaller pieces and use the pieces as accents in a larger project.

INSTANT ABSTRACTS

MATERIALS
Plain shirt (sweatshirt, T-shirt, etc.)
String
Fabric Paint
Piece of cardboard 15" × 25", or big enough to cover your
   working area

PROCEDURE
1. Fold the shirt in half lengthwise to find the center front.
   Reopen.

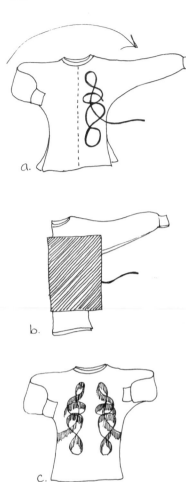

Figure 2.2

2. Soak the string in fabric paint and immediately place it on one half of the shirt front (Figure 2.2a). (Work quickly; the paint is fast drying.) Leave a tail hanging out, away from the shirt.

3. Fold the shirt over the string. Place the piece of cardboard on top of the shirt and hold it in place with the left hand while you pull the string out with your right hand (Figure 2.2b). (Reverse this procedure if you are left-handed.)

4. Remove the cardboard and open the shirt (Figure 2.2c). Nice, huh?

5. Let the shirt dry. Iron on wrong side of the shirt to set the colors.

If you've never painted a fine-art painting, don't be afraid to use a paintbrush—it's only a tool. Get yourself a No. 12 flat brush, dip it in paint, and streak it across the cloth. Pretend you're van Gogh or Kandinsky or Picasso. Did you surprise yourself? I hope so. I know I always do.

Now I'd like you to think about other items that could become paintbrushes. What else might work as a paint applicator? There are sponge brushes, of course. But why not try something new? Feathers, sticks, bingo daubbers, wads of cloth, and bundles of dried corn husks will each provide a totally different effect.

Have you ever tried soaking string in paint, holding the ends tightly, then snapping it? This is the way a carpenter marks a cutting guide with a chalkline. Ideas are everywhere. Keep your eyes open and all of your senses attuned to what's around you.

Painting on Ready-to-Wear

Any of the painting techniques already described can be used on ready-to-wear garments. You just need to work a bit more carefully. You won't be able to cut out only the good parts, as you can with yardage. Freeform abstract designs are the easiest to accomplish. Symmetrical designs, especially those with hard-edged motifs, may make better stencil candidates.

At one time I painted ducks for a well-known carver. The work was in limited-edition collections. This was the first time I had worked on a symmetrical object. What appeared on one side of the bird had to appear on the other side. With the first error I was mortified. How to fix it? You can't erase wood, just as you can't eradicate paint from cloth. The pigment is absorbed into the fibers. The answer from the carver was to make the same "error" on the other side.

I once heard a top runway model say that the irony of modeling is that many designers become known for mistakes that are made by the dressers. Sometimes, unintentionally, the designers create a signature that way. Behind the scenes, a fashion show is fast and hectic with clothes flying everywhere. The dressers work their magic by adapting the clothing to look its best as the models make their entrances onto the stage. A scarf may be put on askew. A section of a dress may be pinned to fit better, thereby changing the drape.

After all, a mistake is just an adaptation or another way to look at something.

Another trick for fabic painting is to use a small square of waxed paper to rest the side of your hand on. It keeps the fabric perfectly clean. Just move the square of paper around as you work. Always keep checking the square for smudges to make sure it hasn't picked up any stray paint. If it has, discard the square and use another. When I am working on a design with small, intricate details, I cut a big stack of the squares and use them throughout the project.

A friend of mine has a great deal of trouble controlling the flow of paint onto the cloth. I suggested the use of resists. A clear resist (available at stores that sell silk painting supplies; see Resources section) is painted or squeezed on the cloth and allowed to dry. Paint then is unable to be absorbed into the cloth wherever the resist was used. Once the garment is painted and dried, the resist is removed in washing.

If you have matte polymer medium on hand, you can use it as a basecoat to control the flow of the paint. Transfer your design to the garment, then paint a basecoat that extends slightly beyond the edges of the design. Paint the design without extending past the polymer painted area. The paint will stay put and not flow into the fibers of the cloth. This method is very useful when painting small intricate motifs.

Working on ready-mades is just as easy as working on whole cloth if you use diligence and forethought. Don't be afraid of the canvas. If you seize up painting picky designs,

> The most famous accident occurred late in the eighteenth century when Lord Spencer (1758–1834) stood too close to a fireplace and burned off his coattails. He liked the tailless coat so much he had short coats intentionally designed for him, hence the birth of the Spencer jacket.

stick with bold abstract expressionism. Throw the paint on the fabric in dribs and dabs. Be free. Express your inner vision.

PAINTING TIPS

- Prewash fabric before painting.
- Any smooth-finished fabric—cotton, broadcloth, duck, denim—is undemanding to paint. Avoid cloth with a textured surface.
- Light-colored fabric can be painted with transluscent or opaque fabric paints. Use opaque paints on dark-colored fabric.
- Once a garment is painted and allowed to dry, turn the piece inside out and iron to set the colors permanently.
- Use squiggle paint to outline painted motifs and add more dimension.
- Use freezer paper as a mask to do simple designs. Cut out the design and iron the remaining freezer paper, waxed side down, onto the garment (Figure 2.3). Using a sponge, brush paint into the open area; use a glitter paint like Starbright. Remove the freezer paper immediately. Let the design dry thoroughly.
- For a hard-edged motif, paint on dry fabric; for a soft watercolor effect, paint on damp cloth. You can also soften the edge of a design by misting it with water immediately after painting it. Work fast, because fabric paint dries quite rapidly.

Figure 2.3

a.

Stenciling

Stenciling is an easy way to approach fabric painting if you are intimidated by a blank canvas. Take a look at the

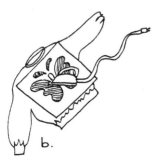

b.

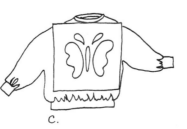

c.

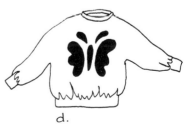

d.

"Starlight" Jacket (Plate 7 in the Color Section); the moons and stars were made with stencils.

A stencil is just a window, a cut-out design, through which you apply fabric paint. You can purchase ready-cut stencils or you can make your own.

TRADITIONAL STENCILING

1. To cut your own designs, you'll need two X-Acto knives: a straight blade for linear cuts and a swivel blade for rounded cuts (Figure 2.4). I use waxed, medium-weight brown vellum for the stencil. Some artists use mylar; others, mat board. Mat board is okay if you plan to make only one or two applications. Otherwise, any soft, absorbent paper should be avoided because it will begin to lose its shape and sharp corners will soon become rounded; eventually your stenciled design will become distorted.
2. To apply the paint, you'll need a stencil brush (see Figure 2.4), a disposable palette, a roll of paper towels, and a jar of water for rinsing your brush.
3. Eject a small dash of paint onto the palette. Using your stencil brush in a vertical position, daub the paint, then hit the brush on the palette to remove excess paint. Still holding your stencil brush in a vertical position, paint the stencil opening from the center to the edges. Rinse your brush thoroughly and wipe with a paper towel before using a different color fabric paint.
4. To do repeats, you'll need to make register marks (Figure 2.5a). Register marks are small holes placed at the corners

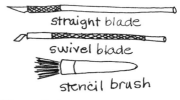

straight blade
swivel blade
stencil brush

Figure 2.4

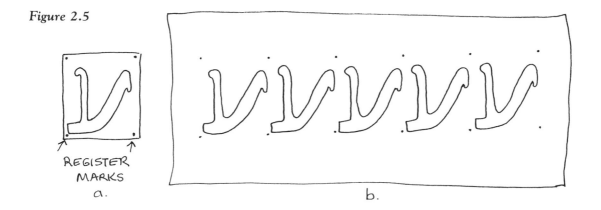

Figure 2.5

REGISTER
MARKS
a.

b.

of the stencil. They are used to line up the design so it is accurately positioned on the cloth. Transfer the register marks onto the cloth with a washable marker so you leave no hint of how you mastered such an exacting job.

5. To use the register marks: Transfer the marks to the cloth and paint the stencil (Figure 2.5b). Remove the stencil and move it to the right. Position the holes on the left side of the stencil so they are lined up with the marks on the cloth that are to the right of the design you just painted. Mark the right two register marks. Paint the stencil. Continue repeating this procedure across the length of the cloth. This same technique can be used to help you line up multicolored designs (Figure 2.6).

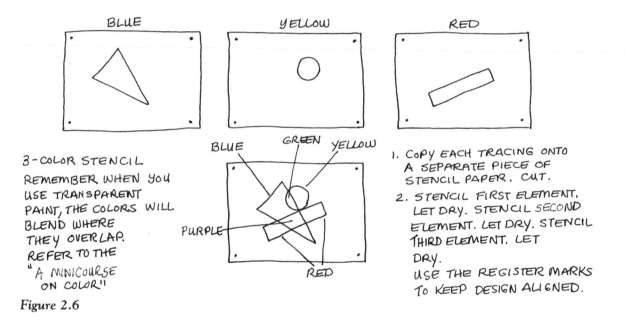

BLUE   YELLOW   RED

BLUE   GREEN   YELLOW

PURPLE   RED

3-COLOR STENCIL

REMEMBER WHEN YOU USE TRANSPARENT PAINT, THE COLORS WILL BLEND WHERE THEY OVERLAP. REFER TO THE "A MINICOURSE ON COLOR"

1. COPY EACH TRACING ONTO A SEPARATE PIECE OF STENCIL PAPER. CUT.

2. STENCIL FIRST ELEMENT. LET DRY. STENCIL SECOND ELEMENT. LET DRY. STENCIL THIRD ELEMENT. LET DRY.
   USE THE REGISTER MARKS TO KEEP DESIGN ALIGNED.

Figure 2.6

NEOSTENCILING

For an even easier method of stenciling, try this.

1. Trace your design onto freezer paper, cut it out, and iron the remaining freezer paper (waxed side down) onto the cloth.

2. Paint the stencil, then remove the paper. You can use this stencil only once, but think of all of the possibilities (Figure 2.7).

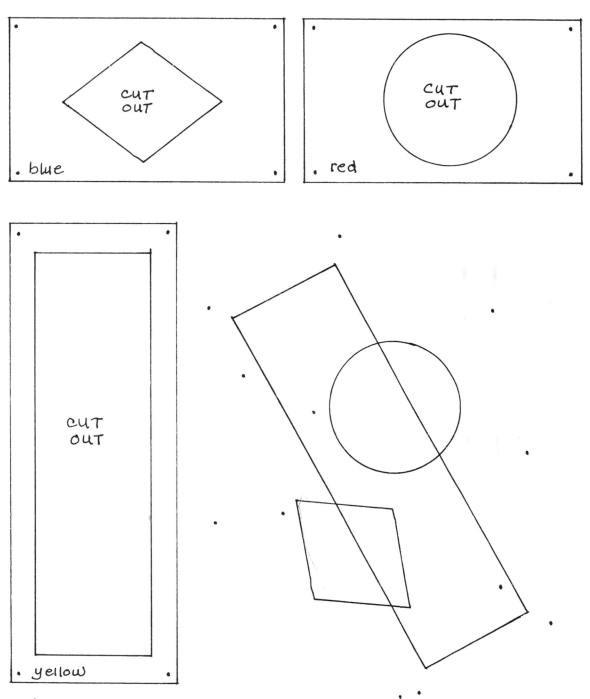

blue

CUT OUT

red

CUT OUT

CUT OUT

yellow

3-COLOR DESIGN

Figure 2.7

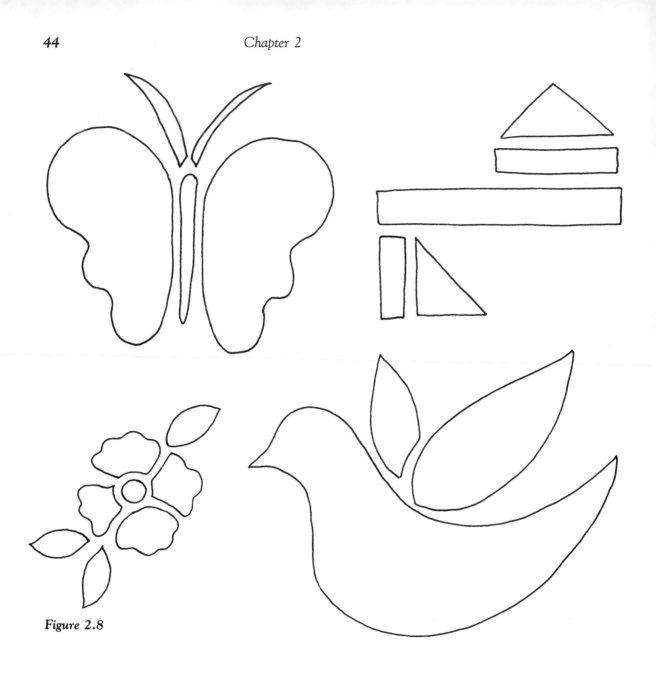

Figure 2.8

Figure 2.8 shows some designs to play with for either method of stenciling.

Stamping

Can't draw? Then this technique is for you.

Have you ever had the opportunity to examine printed textiles in a museum? Did you notice the kimonos emblazoned with repeated motifs of brightly colored fish and golden Japanese mons? These are some of the best examples of fabric stamping.

Stamping is a good way to fill a vast area of blank cloth. A jacket takes anywhere from 3 to 6 yards of fabric and just designing for that much empty space can be intimidating. With stamps you can fill up the field in a relatively short time. First you'll need to select the type of stamps you'll use. Here's what's available (Figure 2.9).

Rubber Stamps

Actually many "rubber" stamps are no longer made of rubber but of a polyresin. Stamps depicting just about any motif you can imagine are available. You can also have stamps of simple, uncluttered designs custom made through stationery stores or print shops. Stamps come unmounted or mounted on wood blocks. You can save money if you mount the rubber stamps, using rubber cement, to your own blocks.

Advantages: Rubber stamps are readily available in lots of designs, including alphabets in different fonts. They also are easy to use.

Disadvantages: Rubber stamps are small and can be expensive.

Figure 2.9

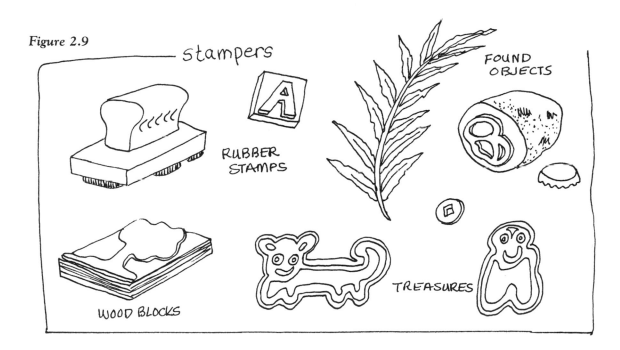

Wood Blocks

Wood blocks for printing are coated with many layers of linoleum. A design is traced onto the surface (remember to reverse any lettering), then the excess linoleum is cut away with special cutting tools.

Advantages: Wood blocks are available in almost every art store and range in size from very small to huge. The design is yours alone.

Disadvantages: You must cut wood blocks yourself, and you need special cutting tools.

Found Objects

Vegetables can be cut in half to reveal the shape of their cross-sections; try green peppers, carrots, broccoli, and apples. Potatoes can be cut with a protruding design. Washers, buttons, bottle caps, kitchen utensils, pressed flowers, ferns, and leaves can also be used. Just look for any flat item that can be mounted to a wooden board or handheld. Then coat the object with paint and print your fabric.

Advantages: Found objects are either free or cost very little; they're available everywhere.

Disadvantages: None.

Treasures

Treasures include hand-carved wooden stamps from India and old rubber stamps from companies that went out of business long ago. Haunt antiques shops and import stores for unusual finds.

Advantages: These items are one-of-a-kind and unusual.

Disadvantages: Unfortunately they can be hard to find.

HOW TO STAMP

1. Cover your work surface with a stack of newspapers. This will protect the tabletop and create a pad that will allow the stamp to print a clearer impression.
2. Place a piece of thick felt (any size that will accommodate the stamp) in an old dish or plastic tray. You will need one piece of felt for each color you wish to print. Saturate each felt piece with fabric paint.
3. Lay prewashed and thoroughly dried fabric flat on the padded work surface.
4. Press the stamp on the felt paint pad and make a sample

imprint on plain paper. If the image is runny, you will need to squeeze some of the paint out of the pad. If some areas of the stamp did not print, check to see if the pad is thoroughly covered with paint. Practice to see the different ways to hold, print, and lift the stamp to achieve the cleanest impression. When the small openings of the stamp start to fill up with paint, take a tiny piece of lint-free cloth, attach it to a toothpick, and remove the paint.

5. Now begin stamping on the cloth. Be sure to wash and dry the stamps when you change colors.
6. Finish stamping and let the cloth dry thoroughly. Iron the wrong side of the cloth to set the paint.
7. Wash off the stamps while the fabric is drying. Make sure they are dry before storing them. Stash the stamps in a dark area; if the stamps are made of rubber, sunlight can deteriorate them.

STAMPING OPTIONS

- Try a fadeaway. Stamp once, then continue stamping without reapplying more paint. The image will become less and less distinct until no image is visible.
- Apply paint directly to the stamp with a paintbrush. Try coloring different sections of the stamp with different colors. You won't have a great deal of time to apply the paint before it dries, so work swiftly in broad swashes of paint rather than little details.
- Press botanicals between sheets of absorbent paper. Weight them down. Remove the flowers and leaves when they are as dry as a cornflake. Glue the botanicals to a wood block and print as usual.
- Use a brayer (small rubber roller, available at art stores) to apply paint to wood blocks.
- Try laying large stamps face up on the work surface, as some stampers prefer to do. Apply the paint, then lay the cloth on the stamp and roll across it with a clean brayer.
- If you are working in a pattern, mark guidelines on the cloth with chalk or a washable marker.
- Work in patterns. Try these: For **flip-flops,** print the image, turn the stamp 180 degrees, and print again (Figure 2.10). For **alternating images,** print the image

Figure 2.10

upright, turn the stamp, and print it upside down (Figure 2.11). **Boxing** involves printing the stamps in a box shape (Figure 2.12). To create **stepping,** print the stamps on an angle (Figure 2.13). To make **mandalas,** print the center motif, then print in circles working outward (Figure 2.14). Be aware of the amount of white

Figure 2.11

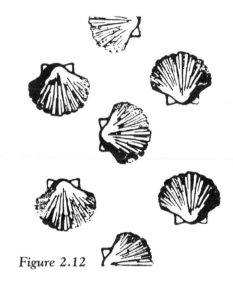

Figure 2.12

Figure 2.13

Figure 2.14

space left between the motifs. This can radically change the total design. Use **white space** creatively. Try no white space, overlapping the images (Figure 2.15). Or add more white space (Figure 2.16).

· Cut your own stamp designs. Figures 2.17 and 2.18 show some ideas to entice your imagination.

Figure 2.16

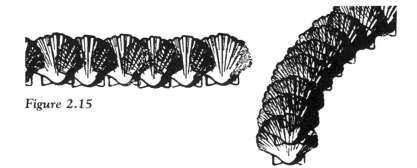

Figure 2.15

Figure 2.17

Figure 2.18

Bleaching

I was first inspired to use bleaching techniques when I saw a quilt made by one of the members of my quilting guild. Her quilt was made of six sections of black rectangles subtly shaded from the darkest ebony black to a soft, sun-faded black. What an interesting effect! I wanted to capture that same effect for inclusion in my own work.

Here are three techniques for bleaching. Be sure to read through all of the instructions and tips before trying the techniques yourself, and remember to cover all your work surfaces with plastic.

SUBTRACTION BLEACHING

I experimented and devised my own technique to recreate the gradated effect in the quilt I'd seen.

1. I filled my washer with water as usual, then I added half a gallon of bleach.
2. Because my washer cycle is 20 minutes, I added a large square of 100% cotton cloth every 4 minutes. This resulted in five squares of cloth in a nicely gradated color tone.
3. When I was done, I added one unbleached cloth square to make a six-square run.

Try using this subtraction bleaching technique on any dark, color-soaked cotton cloth.

DIRECT BLEACHING

Another bleaching application is the direct method.

1. Fill a spray bottle with bleach and use it to spritz the fabric.
2. Concentrate the spray in some areas and leave some parts untouched. This creates a mottling effect.

TIE-DYE BLEACHING

The last method is an adaption of a tie-dye technique.

1. Lay a piece of fabric out flat, then fold it into evenly spaced sections, as if you were making a paper fan (Figure 2.19). Pin the folds to hold them in place.

Figure 2.19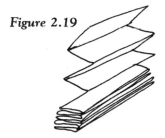

2. Then, using a long basting stitch, sew the pleats together about ½" from the outside edge of either side (Figure 2.20).

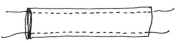

Figure 2.20

3. Fill a basin with 2" of bleach. Fold the fabric to fit within the dimensions of the basin. Dip the edges of the cloth in bleach until the color starts to loosen and color the liquid (Figure 2.21). You can remove the fabric at this point or let it soak longer for more color removal. Repeat for the other edge of the cloth.

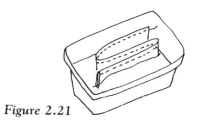

Figure 2.21

Figure 2.22

4. When you've finished dipping the cloth, wash the cloth to remove the bleach. Remove the basting threads and you'll have an interesting striped, ombré-like design (Figure 2.22). How would that work on some of that ho-hum cloth you have?

Think about other ways you could use the bleach. What about knotting the fabric before bleaching? How about using different dilutions: half strength or quarter strength?

BLEACHING TIPS

- Bleach is a potent chemical. It can eat right through cloth if it's left in contact with it for too long. Thoroughly rinse any fabric after the bleaching process.
- Set the final color by immersing the cloth in a 15-minute acid soak made of water and vinegar in a two-to-one ratio.
- Wear gloves when working with chemicals such as bleach.
- Have adequate ventilation. Open your windows and turn on the exhaust fan. Better yet; work outdoors.

- Because bleach reacts differently on different types of cloth, experiment with small 4″ squares before attempting a large project.
- Keep a record of your experiments in a notebook or on your computer. You can refer back to it and save yourself time and frustration.

BLEACHING OPTION

- Try some of the discharge/disperse dyes. I have used them with uneven results but they are necessary for overdyeing procedures.

Marbling

Have you admired the handsome marbled end papers of fine books? The same effect can be translated to cloth with a few modifications.

Traditional marbling is based on the principle that oil and water don't mix. Essentially, thinned oil paint is floated on a water surface, then transferred to paper.

There are at least two ways to accomplish this with fabric—one with oil paint, the other with water-based fabric paint. With either method, the cloth should first be prepared with a mordant solution to allow the paint to penetrate the fibers of the cloth, creating a permanent adhesion.

To mordant the cloth, thoroughly wet the cloth in tepid water and wring out. In a large plastic dishpan add 3 tablespoons alum (available at supermarkets, in the spice section) for each quart of warm water. Soak the damp cloth in the alum/water mixture for 1 hour.

Remove the cloth, wring it out, and hang it to dry. Do not rinse the mordant from the fabric. It will be removed after the painting process.

MARBLING METHOD # 1

The design on the "Marble Bag" shown in Plate 3 of the Color Section was accomplished by this oil paint–based method of marbling.

MATERIALS
Oil paint
Turpentine
Large pizza pan or butcher's tray
Cloth (be sure to mordant the cloth as described earlier in this
    section, p. 54)
Manipulators, such as pencils, sticks, saw blades, and combs
Large plastic garbage bag
Old newspapers

PROCEDURE
1. Fill a shallow basin with water.
2. Thin the oil paints with turpentine to a thick, but pourable
   consistency.
3. Drizzle the paint on the surface of the water. Add as many
   different colors as you choose. Slowly swirl the paint to
   blend some areas. For swirling tools you can use tongue
   depressors, sticks, plastic spoons, or a similar utensil. One
   of the most intriguing tools is a comb. Buy a large-toothed
   plastic comb and remove every other tooth. Lightly drag
   the comb through the suspended paint. The result is as-
   tounding: pointed swirls in a quasi-ogee pattern.
4. To print, lay the cloth on the surface and immediately remove. Place the cloth, design side up, on a plastic garbage bag to dry.
5. Once the cloth is thoroughly dry, it can be laundered and
   used as regular cloth. Don't worry, no odor will remain in
   the cloth.
6. To continue marbling, first remove the paint design by laying a sheet of newspaper on the water surface. The newspaper will pick up the excess paint, leaving a pristine surface for your next marble design. Discard the wet
   newspaper and begin again from Step #3.

Strict rules for dressing by social class were prevalent in colonial America. If you dressed in clothing considered to be better than your station in life, you would be publicly flogged and would have to pay a fine!

   The second method of marbling uses the popular water-
soluble fabric paints. Because the "oil and water don't mix"
maxim doesn't apply to these paints, we need to find a way
to suspend the paint. I have used three different media: liquid carageenan (available through mail-order sources listed in
the Resources section of this book), liquid starch, and wallpaper paste. Marbling using this method will produce different

results from Marbling Method #1, even if you use the same type of cloth. With either method, remember that a solid white cotton will look more luminous, whereas an unbleached muslin will absorb the light and reflect a soft, matte appearance. Also check the recommendations from the fabric paint manufacturer; some paints adhere better to a polycotton blend.

MARBLING METHOD #2

MATERIALS
Fabric paint
Wide, shallow container
Carageenan (see Resources at the back of the book)
Cloth (be sure to mordant the cloth, as described earlier in this
    section)
Manipulators, such as pencils, sticks, saw blades, and combs
Large plastic garbage bag

PROCEDURE
1. Mix 2½ teaspoons of carageenan powder in 1 gallon of warm water. Either place the mixture in a blender or beat it with a wire whisk. Dissolve as much of the powder as possible. If a few bits of powder remain unmixed, it's okay. Pour the suspension liquid into a shallow 13″ × 15″ pan. The liquid gel will be approximately 1¼″ deep. Let the carageenan sit overnight or at least 12 hours. Remove any bubbles that may have formed on the surface.

2. Sprinkle paint on surface. Disturb the surface with sticks or other manipulators to whirl the paint in an attractive pattern. Don't overwork it or the colors will become muddy and drop.

3. Carefully lay the cloth on the paint surface. Pull up the cloth and lay it right side up on a plastic garbage bag to dry. Don't try to hold up the cloth before it is dry or the colors will run together and ruin the marbled design.

4. Once the fabric is thoroughly dry, rinse and dry it again. Iron the marbled cloth on the wrong side to further set the color.

5. Two other media for suspending the fabric paint can be used: wallpaper paste (mix according to manufacturer's in-

structions) and liquid starch used straight from the bottle. Experiment—each medium produces a somewhat different effect. Figure 2.23a is the result of a wide-toothed comb drawn through the paint. To create a stone pattern like the one shown in Figure 2.23b, use an eye dropper to drop the paint onto the surface. The effect in Figure 2.23c can be achieved by dropping paint onto the surface and then manipulating it with a stick.

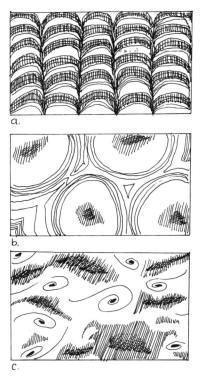

Marbling looks excellent on solid-colored cloth, but feel free to experiment on some of the unwanted, preprinted fabric you already own. I really like the outcome of marbling on tiny, too fussy florals and fabric with out-of-date coloring.

When you select colors for marbling, remember the color wheel and the way the colors will mix when manipulated. For example, if you use yellow and blue paint and swirl them together, you will also have green in your design where they meet. Refer to "A Mini-Course on Color" in Chapter 1 if you have trouble recalling the color mixes you can achieve.

Figure 2.23

Blueprinting and Brownprinting

The "Wildflorist Shirt" shown in Plate 5 of the Color Section is a good example of how to incorporate blueprinted cloth into your art-to-wear garments. This T-top also includes marbling and other hand-dyed fabrics. This piece was made almost 10 years ago, and the colors are still true. The only care needed has been an occasional hand wash and line dry.

Blueprinting on cloth offers a wide range of possibilities, resulting in an exciting and beautiful fabric-printing statement. The process is relatively simple, but does warrant caution, since you are using potentially hazardous chemicals. Keep children and pets away and always wear rubber gloves.

Basically, sensitized fabric is exposed in the sun or with photo flood lights to create a positive image similar to a blueprint of house plans. The imagery is produced by any object you lay on the cloth to block out the sun's (or lights') ultraviolet rays. This process is known as creating a "photogram."

BLUEPRINTING PROCESS

Here's the basic recipe. Please read through the entire process before beginning. Be sure to mix the solutions in a darkened room.

1. For **Solution A,** add 2 ounces of ferric ammonium citrate to 1 cup of water. For **Solution B,** add 1 ounce of potassium ferricyanide to 1 cup of water.

2. These chemicals are light reactive and should be stored in amber bottles. I used quart-size beer bottles with corks for stoppers. Label each bottle with masking tape marked "Solution A" and "Solution B." Mix by gently shaking each bottle. The chemicals must be fully dissolved to obtain a good print. When the chemicals are mixed with water they will remain active for 3 to 4 months. Once the solutions have been mixed together they will be potent for 5 to 6 hours.

3. In a large enamel pan, mix equal parts of Solution A and Solution B together. (Remember this process must be done in a darkened room.) Use a stick or dowel to mix. Do not use any cooking utensils or you will have to dispose of them after use. Using prewashed and dried cloth, soak the cloth in the mixture and let the excess run back into the pan, then hang the cloth to dry. Repeat for the rest of the cloth. If you are unable to print right away, store treated cloth in a black plastic bag for up to 6 months. I used cotton for the "Wildflorist Shirt" but have also had good results with rayon. Don't be afraid to experiment; satin would be an interesting choice. The only type of fabric I would foresee problems with would be a napped fabric such as corduroy.

4. Have a piece of ¼" plywood and a piece of Plexiglas (or a piece of glass with the edges taped to prevent cuts) cut to the same dimensions. Place the sensitized cloth on the plywood. Now select the object, or objects, you wish to print. Anything that obstructs light will work. Try lace, weeds, leaves, paper cutouts, hardware goods (nuts, bolts, saw blades, etc.). Or you may wish to print an enlarged photo negative. Anything that is relatively flat and thin will give a clear image.

5. Once you are satisfied with the arrangement of the objects on the cloth, place the piece of Plexiglas over the

cloth and carry the "photogram sandwich" outside to expose it in the sun. Exposure time will depend a great deal on atmospheric conditions. My exposure time here in northern Illinois has run from 3 to 15 minutes. The image will develop right before your eyes, so use your own judgment.

6. When finished exposing, undo the assembly and wash the cloth in running water until the water is clear. Dry the cloth, then press it as usual. No further fixing is necessary.

7. From personal experience, I would suggest not printing on a humid day. Humidity wreaks havoc with the process by fogging the print. Also select a day with low wind.

There are many variables when working with this process so use the recipe given only as a guide. You can create your own personal formula by varying the chemical amounts, exposure times, and type of cloth used. Keep a record of solutions and exposures for personal reference.

BLUEPRINTING TIPS

- Dispose of any unused solutions safely. (Check with your local recyclers for recommendations.)
- Clean out the dye pot and rinse all utensils and mark them "Use for Dyeing Only."

If you are interested in trying blueprinted cloth but don't want to fuss with the chemicals you can buy presensitized fabric squares and T-shirts from Blueprint-Printables, listed in Resources, later in the book.

The brownprinting process is used in a similar fashion as the blueprinting process. The final print is a bit less dramatic and has a more nostalgic appeal.

BROWNPRINTING PROCESS

1. In a darkened room: Mix 1¾ ounces of ferric ammonium citrate with 1 cup of water. Mix 1¾ ounces of tartaric acid with 1 cup of water. Mix these solutions together. Then

mix 1 ounce of silver nitrate (Caution: Can stain and burn!), with 1 cup of water. Add the silver nitrate solution very slowly to the previous solution so all three solutions are now mixed. Soak the fabric in the solution for 5 minutes and hang to dry. Now you can print the sensitized cloth following Steps #4 and #5 in "Blueprinting Process."

2. After printing, rinse the cloth in running water to remove the chemicals. To bring up the image, you must immerse the cloth in a "hypo." Mix 1 part sodium thiosulfate with 20 parts water. Briefly dip the entire cloth in the solution. Work fast. As soon as you see the color change (this happens in less than 1 minute) remove the cloth or the image will disappear entirely! Finally rinse the cloth to remove all chemicals. Then hang it to dry.

COMMERCIAL ALTERNATIVE METHOD

If you'd rather not work with heavy-duty chemicals, you might like to try Inko light-sensitive dyes.

1. Lay fabric flat on a covered work surface.
2. Arrange flattened ferns, other botanicals, or paper cutouts on the cloth (the covered areas will remain the color of the fabric).
3. Place blue Inko dye in a spray bottle and spritz the fabric. Remove the objects and let the cloth dry flat. This method is a "kissin' cousin" to blueprinting.

*L*eaf Printing

Gardening and a healthy respect for nature are my other passions. Often I will find design elements on my daily walks. Some may be as abstract as the raindrops on a leaf of lady's-mantle or the tidal pattern around a stray piece of driftwood. Others are more concrete in their design pattern. Leaves are one example. Leaves come in various shapes and sizes, useful in any project you may be working on. Simply press leaves between sheets of absorbent paper (an old telephone book works well) and weight them down for a month, and you'll have material to work with year-round.

LEAF INSPIRATION

- Trace around the leaf for a perfect pattern.
- Use the leaves for blueprinting. I made a quilt titled "Herbal Album" using the herbs I grow in my garden.
- Try a product called Design Dye, which comes in sheets of many colors. You simply iron the color sheet to the leaf, remove the paper, then iron the colored leaf to fabric. Design Dye is available from Swanco Industrial (see Resources, at the back of the book).

BASIC LEAF PRINTING

This method of leaf printing transfers the actual juices of the plant into the fabric (kind of like grass stains on the knees of a kid's pants, only this is intentional!).

1. First mordant the fabric by dissolving 3 tablespoons of alum (available in supermarkets, in the spice section) in 1 quart of warm water. Soak the fabric in the alum/water mix for 15 minutes. Do not rinse; just hang to dry.
2. When the fabric is completely dry, go outside and collect the fresh leaves you want to print. Lay the fabric on a stack of newspapers to create a pad. Place a leaf on the fabric and cover this with another piece of mordanted cloth. Take a rubber mallet and pound the "sandwich" to make the leaf print. Finish printing the rest of the leaves.
3. Remove any leaf residue and let the prints dry. Iron on both sides to further fix the print. You now can use the fabric as usual. It can be laundered in mild detergent.

Image Transfers

Have you ever paged through a magazine or catalog and run across an illustration that you loved? Now you can capture that picture on cloth. Actually this method has been around for a while. I first used it 15 years ago when decoupage was being taught in crafts shops everywhere. I did a lamp base with a cutout illustration. What is fresh about the technique is that we can now apply it to cloth.

Any illustration on any kind of paper (slick magazine

pages, newspapers, flyers, etc.) will work. You can even transfer old photographs without damaging the original. Just take the photographs to a printer who has a 4-color copier and make a print. You can then transfer off of the copy you made. Black-and-white photos can be copied on a regular paper copier. *Caution:* any lettering will be reversed when transferred.

Many people use this image transfer process to create ancestor quilts, but the possibilities are endless. Transfer an illustration to your denim jacket, the pocket of a classic white shirt, children's clothes, or costumes.

MAKING AN IMAGE TRANSFER

MATERIALS
Illustration on paper
Matte polymer medium (available at art- or crafts-supply stores)
Large paintbrush
Waxed paper
White 100% cotton cloth (you can transfer an image to cloth
    and then appliqué it to a garment or transfer directly to the
    garment)

PROCEDURE
1. Cover your work surface with waxed paper.
2. Coat the cotton fabric with polymer medium, using a large paintbrush or a foam paint pad; be generous.
3. Coat the illustration you wish to transfer with the medium. Next, lay the image face-side down on the prepared cotton fabric. Smooth out the illustration, and coat it with another layer of polymer medium (Figure 2.24). Let the polymer medium dry 24 or more hours.
4. Lay the cotton cloth image in a bowl or basin of tepid water (be careful not to scrunch the fabric) and soak for 1 hour.
5. After the fabric has soaked, use your fingers to begin scrubbing away the paper. Use a firm touch, but don't be too rough or you will break through the illustration. Continue scrubbing until all of the paper is removed. Voilà! The image is permanently transferred to the fabric. Let the cloth dry, and iron from the back to further set the inks.

Figure 2.24

IMAGE-TRANSFER OPTIONS

- Make an entire collage using cutouts from magazines. If the illustration has lettering, remember it will reverse in printing. If the message is important, your printer can make a reverse image. This is somewhat expensive so save it for important projects.
- Seek out the polymer medium in a gloss form. Try it for a slightly different look.
- Design your own transfers by arranging a bunch of collage items on the photocopier. The items should be flat so you can close the copier lid. Lay them directly on the glass and make copies.
- Start an illustration morgue. A morgue is simply a collection of photos or illustrations kept in a file for future use. Use a cardboard box and make some dividers with labels so you can find the items you want when you want them. The categories in my file include angels, art deco, art nouveau, neo-modern, goddesses, interesting geometrics, wild stuff, and miscellaneous good stuff.
- Try this technique for transferring black-and-white copies to cloth: Place the copy face down on the cloth and iron, using the cotton setting and heavy pressure.
- Try the new transfer papers made specifically for photocopiers (both black-and-white and color).

3 *Manipulations*

"There is nothing new under the sun" as the old saying goes. And that is true. Most of the sewing techniques used in this book have been around for centuries. Early clothing was loose and drapey. The Greeks were the first to actually mold the clothing to the individual wearer (an old form of tailoring known as the "seventh-century fit"). Clothing side slits are seen in early Italian paintings of nymphs. Quilting appeared in the thirteenth century in the form of a padded doublet made to be worn under metal armor. Ribbon weaving was first reported in France in the mid–fourteenth century, and slashing appeared in the sixteenth century, primarily in shirts worn by wealthy men.

What is new and refreshing is the application. We have found numerous ways to adjust and acclimate these ancient techniques to fit our modern sense of style and our fast-paced schedules. With the invention and ever-improving technology of the sewing machine, serger, and other tools, we can create enchanting garments within a brief span of time.

We no longer sew out of necessity. In fact, with the buying power of the huge franchises, I doubt you could sew a garment for less than you could buy it. Garment-making is no longer the penny-pinching measure it once was. Now we have the luxury of sewing for other reasons, a major impetus being our need to express our individuality. Furthermore, we can show our mastery of sewing skills without saying "homemade." Our clothing looks professional.

Each technique in *Embellishments* is explained with modern methods. In addition to the instructions, tips are often provided to help you master the technique. Then, to take the technique even further, options are listed. These are creative ideas meant to help you use the technique even more artistically. My wish is to get you to think of surprising ways to work artistically. I'm positive you will come up with some great ideas of your own.

Throughout the book I give you many design motifs. Feel free to take a design from one section and use it with a different technique. You'll want to keep samples of each of the techniques you try. They'll be especially valuable in putting together the "Oo-La-La Jacket" in Chapter 5.

Happy exploration!

Appliqué

If you are new to sewing and need to find one outstanding technique, appliqué is it. Appliqué can turn an ordinary garment into a masterpiece. Whether you sew your own clothing or purchase your wardrobe, you can add appliqué.

The term "appliqué" refers to a piece of cloth attached to whole cloth by either a machine satin stitch or invisibly by hand. The appliqué pieces can be motifs cut from printed cloth, such as a flower, or they can be designs cut out of cloth into a recognizable or abstract shape. You could cut out a sailboat to apply to a garment with a nautical theme. Abstract shapes can be geometrics like squares, circles, and triangles, or be totally free-form.

APPLIQUÉ PRELIMINARIES

There are a few essentials to perfect appliqué.

1. Use a fusing material to adhere the appliqué to the ground fabric. It looks much more professional . . . no puckers or misalignment.
2. Wash all fabric before you appliqué it to a wash-and-wear garment. Otherwise the appliqué fabric may shrink in laundering and ruin the garment.
3. Match the garment fabrics. Use dry-clean-only fabrics like velvet and fine satin on dry-clean-only garments. Use washable fabrics together (cottons with cottons, etc.).
4. Match the thread color with the appliqué for an invisible look. Or accent the appliqué with contrasting color thread, which is usually done with a metallic thread.

5. If you make a mistake, use the seam ripper from the back of the garment and remove threads from the front with a piece of Scotch tape.

BASIC APPLIQUÉ BY MACHINE

1. Fuse the fabric to paper-backed fusible web like Wonder-Under. Cut out the appliqué. Remove the backing sheet, and iron it in place on the garment.
2. Set the sewing machine for satin stitch. A short stitch length with a wide width is the typical satin stitch, but you can use a narrow to very wide width to suit your particular project. The widest width works best on straight-edged designs like rectangles. The narrower widths look more professional and are easier to accomplish. Turning corners is much simpler with the narrow width.
3. Test the stitch on scrap fabric of the same weight as the cloth you will be appliquéing. Adjust the machine's tension correctly. Then set the stitch length, which will create the density of stitches. When the stitches are not very dense, there will be too much space between them (Figure 3.1a), indicating the stitch is too long and you should decrease the stitch length. If the stitching is too dense, the thread will overlap (Figure 3.1b), and you should increase the stitch length. The perfect stitch is shown in Figure 3.1c.
4. Fuse a generous piece of freezer wrapping paper to the wrong side of the garment beneath the appliqué. This further stabilizes the design and allows for a finer satin stitch. The paper has a tendency to dull your needle, so put in a fresh needle when you start an appliqué project.
5. Begin stitching in an area where the start and finish of your work won't show (Figure 3.2). Usually an inside cor-

Figure 3.1

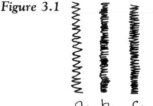

a. b. c.

Figure 3.2

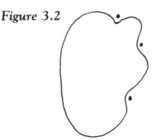

START APPLIQUE AT ANY OF THE DOTS

ner is a good spot. Don't begin in the middle of a long
straight area.

6. To turn outside corners, take one stitch past the edge of
the appliqué (Figure 3.3). Insert the needle on the outside
edge so the needle will swing back on the appliqué. Raise
the presser foot and pivot the cloth. Continue sewing.

Figure 3.3

★ TURNING OUTSIDE CORNERS

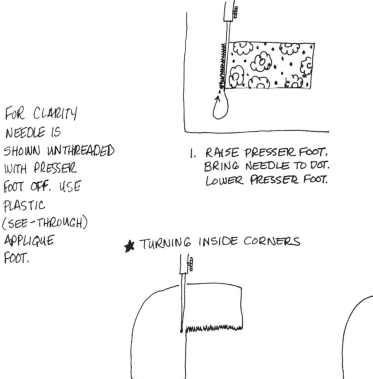

FOR CLARITY
NEEDLE IS
SHOWN UNTHREADED
WITH PRESSER
FOOT OFF. USE
PLASTIC
(SEE-THROUGH)
APPLIQUE
FOOT.

1. RAISE PRESSER FOOT,
BRING NEEDLE TO DOT.
LOWER PRESSER FOOT.

2. CONTINUE SEWING.

★ TURNING INSIDE CORNERS

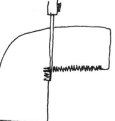

1. RAISE PRESSER FOOT.
BRING NEEDLE TO DOT.
LOWER PRESSER FOOT.

2. CONTINUE SEWING.

7. To turn inside corners, stitch past the end to the width of
the appliqué stitch (Figure 3.3). Take one stitch to put the
needle on the inside edge of the corner. Raise the presser
foot and pivot the cloth. Continue sewing.

Figure 3.4

8. End the stitching by taking three stitches in place. Or you can thread a needle, take the thread to the back of the garment, and knot. Trim the extra thread away with sharp scissors. Remove the freezer paper from the back of the garment.

Figure 3.4 provides a few appliqué motifs you can try.

PADDED APPLIQUÉ

If you want a puffy, three-dimensional look to your appliqué, try padding it.

1. Simply cut a piece of fusible batting a tiny bit smaller then the appliqué piece. Draw around the appliqué on the garment for perfect placement.
2. Fuse the batting in place, then fuse the appliqué in place on top of the batting (Figure 3.5). Appliqué as directed in "Basic Appliqué by Machine."

Figure 3.5

SHADOW WORK

This technique looks somewhat like appliqué but is really a different technique. Brightly colored cotton fabric motifs are sandwiched between a backing cloth and a sheer top layer. The finished garment looks like there are subtle jewels embedded in the cloth. Here's how to do it.

1. Fuse the cloth for the design motifs to paper-backed fusible web like Wonder-Under. Cut the motifs exactly to size. No seam allowance is needed. Iron the motifs in place on a solid-colored background.

2. Place a piece of sheer (see-through) fabric, such as batiste or fine handkerchief linen, over the motif (Figure 3.6).

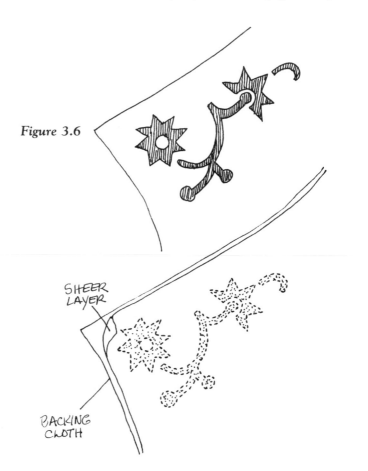

Figure 3.6

SHEER LAYER

BACKING CLOTH

3. Thread a needle and use a quilting stitch to sew around the design motifs. Tie the thread off on the back of the backing cloth. The thread can be white or you can use a thread color to match the design motif. You can also sew around by machine (free-machine stitching is easiest).

PROGRESSION APPLIQUÉ

Anytime you make multipiece appliqués, you will need to sew them onto the backing fabric in order. The progression runs from the back to the front. For an example, look at the floral appliqué in Figure 3.7.

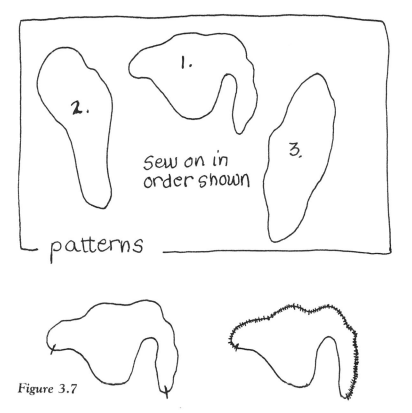

Figure 3.7

1. The design is made up of three pieces.
2. Fuse all three pieces to paper-backed fusible web like Wonder-Under. You may want to pad Piece 3 with batting to give it more shape.
3. Piece 1 is fused onto the backing first. Lay the other two pieces in place and mark what parts of Piece 1 will show. Remove Pieces 2 and 3. Appliqué Piece 1 just a bit beyond the marks so the end of the stitching won't show. You don't need to sew on parts that will be covered.
4. Position Piece 2 in place. Set Piece 3 over it and mark. Remove Piece 3. Sew along the edges of Piece 2, except where it will be covered by Piece 3. Finally, sew Piece 3 in place.

One of the advantages of being a part of a guild is that everyone willingly shares knowledge. Try this wonderful tech-

nique I learned from my guild for making stems and other
linear designs. I use it extensively in quilts and on clothing.

HOLLY'S APPLIQUÉD STEMS

1. Take a strip of cloth four times the width of the desired
   finished stem and fold in half with the lower edge slightly
   protruding (this is to ensure you catch the lower layer
   when you sew) (Figure 3.8).

Figure 3.8

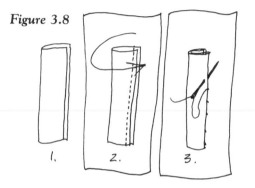

1.   2.   3.

2. Place the piece on the backing. Sew a line of stitching
   slightly in from the raw edge.
3. Roll the folded edge over just beyond the raw edge and
   appliqué it in place.
4. This makes a beautifully puffed stem and has a very professional look. I even used this technique in a very contemporary quilt to make sharp action lines that accentuated a
   glowing urn.

Figure 3.9

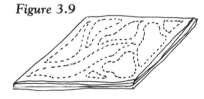

CUT-AWAY APPLIQUÉ

If you are looking for an interesting technique that works up a
lot of texture, try this.

1. Stack layers of different types of fabric in different colors.
   Loosely baste them together or simply hold them in place
   if you are creating a small piece (Figure 3.9).
2. Using a straight machine stitch, sew amorphous, free-form
   closed shapes.
3. Then take sharp scissors and begin cutting away layers inside your stitched designs. In some of the shapes cut

down only one layer to expose the second cloth; in other areas cut farther down to expose the deeper layers.

4. Now go back to your machine and sew a satin stitch over the exposed cloth edges. Embellish further with beads or other trinkets.

With cut-away appliqué you can achieve different effects by using different cloth—matte, shiny, opaque, sheer. And you can change the color effect by using all soft pastels or bold, clashing colors.

Patchwork

I'm convinced good tools are worth their weight in gold. I remember the pre-rotary cutter days when we cut out our patches with scissors. Sometimes the pieces wouldn't quite fit together properly. Those days are gone. With the manufacture of many tools specifically created for the quiltmaker, patchwork is now a pleasure. The accuracy you can attain is amazing. Everything works!

Here is a list of the tools I consider essential:

Rotary Cutter. Buy the large, heavy-duty size, which can cut through ten layers of cloth with precision (Figure 3.10). Rotary cutters are also available in a smaller size and in a double-bladed version.

Self-Healing Mat. This is a necessity for using with the rotary cutter, otherwise you'll damage the table surface you are working on (Figure 3.10). The cut marks in the mat repair themselves.

Thread Snips. These are for snipping away stray threads as you sew (Figure 3.11).

Figure 3.10

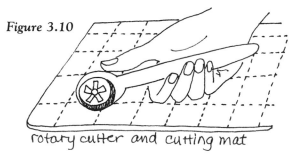

rotary cutter and cutting mat

thread snips

Figure 3.11

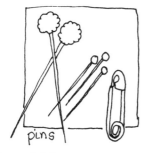

Figure 3.12

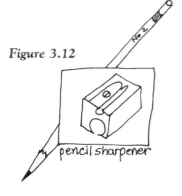

In 1846 both Elias Howe and Issac Singer, independently of each other, came out with the first primitive versions of the sewing machine.

Figure 3.13

Figure 3.14

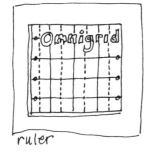

Metal Pencil Sharpener. Metal sharpeners sharpen much better than plastic ones and don't eat your marking pencils (Figure 3.12).

Pencils. You'll need a light-colored pencil for marking dark fabrics and a medium-toned one for light fabrics.

Straight Pins. Use 1¾" quilting pins and shorter 1" ball-headed pins (Figure 3.13).

Safety Pins. Use these for basting the layers together.

Omnigrid Ruler. The 6" × 24" size is the most versatile (Figure 3.14). I also like the 6" square for smaller projects.

Patchwork is a truly American art form that evolved from necessity. When the cost of fabric was dear, our foremothers created quilts from the scraps leftover from garment-making. As a garment was outgrown, it became a candidate for patchwork pieces, too.

Late twentieth-century quilt making is radically different from those early days in colonial America. Today we buy new cloth specifically for an entire project, and then we are likely to add further embellishment, like beads and buttons, as nonfunctioning adornments. Today anything goes, from purely decorative work to faithful reproductions of traditional quilts with intriguing names like Wild Goose Chase, Jacob's Ladder, Orange Peel, Delectable Mountains, Dove in the Window, and Rocky Road to California.

Patchwork has memorialized everything from births, marriages, and deaths to political messages, favorite flowers, and contemporary color scales.

My patchwork began quite simply with a quilt of 4" squares for my son (who is now 21). From there, I experimented with other geometric shapes—triangles, rectangles, hexagons, and diamonds (singly and in combination). Appliqué became my all-time favorite for many years. Now, once again, I am back to the simple shapes, especially the square, using color as the important feature on which to build interest within the design.

HOW TO SEW SIMPLE PATCHWORK USING 100% COTTON

1. Using the Omnigrid ruler, rotary cutter, and mat, cut strips; then slice off a stack of squares. The size is up to you.

2. Place two squares flush, right sides facing, and sew them together along one side (Figure 3.15). Usually a ¼" seam allowance is used in patchwork, but you can use any seam allowance, as long as you use it consistently throughout your work.

3. Open up the two sewn squares. Place a third square, right sides facing, along one of the squares and sew it in place. Continue adding squares until you reach the desired width for your quilt or garment. (One garment example is the "Chroma" coat in the Color Section.)

4. Make as many strips as you'll need, then sew the strips of patchwork together to create whole cloth. Iron the piece.

SLICE-AND-DICE PATCHWORK

1. Create a large piece of square patchwork either in a staggered pattern (such as Trip Around the World) or randomly placed squares (Figure 3.16).

Figure 3.15

Figure 3.16

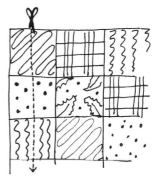

Figure 3.17

2. Cut the patchwork apart down the center of a section of squares. Do not cut on the seam line. I find it easier to cut down the length than down the width. Figure 3.17 shows the cutting line down the left side.

3. Cut a strip of cloth the length of the whole patchwork cloth (Figure 3.18). The width of the strip is up to you. I use a 3" strip on a cloth made of 5" squares. Sew the strip of cloth between the patchwork pieces you cut apart, making sure the horizontal seams of the patchwork on each side of the strip are lined up. The patchwork squares

Figure 3.18

↥ strip added

Figure 3.19

on either side of the fabric strip are now matching half squares (Figure 3.19).

4. Now cut apart the patchwork on the right side and sew in another strip of cloth.
5. Cut across the quilt in the opposite direction and sew in another strip. Then cut across another row parallel to it and add a fourth strip. Figure 3.20 gives an example.
6. Continue cutting and adding strips as desired. The result is a patchwork that looks very complicated and attractive. All of the half squares will have mirror images on the other side of the fabric strips.

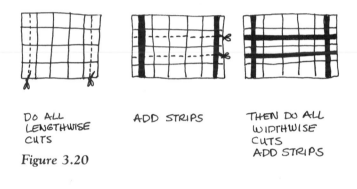

DO ALL   ADD STRIPS   THEN DO ALL
LENGTHWISE   WIDTHWISE
CUTS   CUTS
                                    ADD STRIPS

Figure 3.20

Some other examples of slice-and-dice patchwork, showing different-width strips, can be seen in Figures 3.21, 3.22, and 3.23.

Figure 3.21

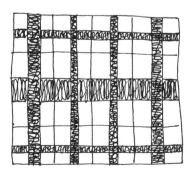

Figure 3.22

Figure 3.23

SLICE-AND-DICE TIPS

- Don't iron your garment or quilt before erasing the marking lines. The heat from the iron can set the inks of some markers.
- Press the seams on patchwork to one side.
- Press, press, press for a professional finished product. Many times I will take my garments to the cleaners for a professional pressing.
- Invest in a steamer. You can take out the wrinkles without smashing the nap of the cloth.
- When combining two different types of cloth (say velvet and brocade), sew with strips of tear-away stabilizer underneath the cloth. It will prevent distortion.
- Cut strips of cloth lengthwise to the grain of the cloth. The warp is firmer than the weft threads and produces a more stable piece of cloth. If you cut strips crosswise to the grain, the patchwork is more stretchy and can bow in the final piece.

SLICE-AND-DICE OPTION

- Try chaining to create your patchwork base. Stitch squares together in long strips by sewing without lifting the presser foot (Figure 3.24). Place two squares together, right sides facing, on the bed of the sewing machine and sew them together at one edge. Stop when you have gone about three-quarters of the length of the square, and place two more squares behind the first set,

Figure 3.24

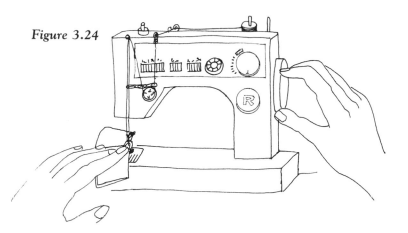

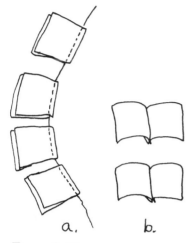

Figure 3.25

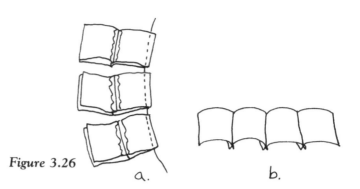

Figure 3.26

abutting the sets at the edges. Continue sewing and adding pairs of squares (Figure 3.25a). Remove the chain of squares from the machine, clip the squares apart, and open up each set (Figure 3.25b). Now you are ready to sew the sets together using the same method (Figure 3.26). You can create chained sets of 2, 4, 8, or 16 squares. This is an especially easy method for creating random patchwork. If you are working with a distinct pattern like Trip Around the World, lay all of the squares out on the floor, then gather them together carefully so you can sew them precisely as they have been laid out. Sometimes making a simple chart on graph paper aids in maintaining the sequence.

PICK-UP STICKS

Another way to make interesting slice-and-dice cloth is to make what I call "pick-up sticks." Here's how to do it:

1. Lay yardage out flat and plan your design. Figure 3.27a shows one prospect.
2. Use a steel yardstick and cut across the cloth with a rotary cutter (Figure 3.27b).
3. Cut a strip of cloth (the width of the strip is up to you) and sew it back into the yardage (Figure 3.27c).
4. Cut through the yardage again, perhaps at an angle, and sew in another strip (Figure 3.27d). Continue slicing and sewing in strips. If you don't match up the fabric on either side of the strips, you will end up with an interesting fracturing or offset effect. Visually the strips will not line up across the cloth. This can be just as pleasing as the look of strips that are more precisely matched.

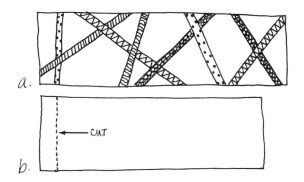
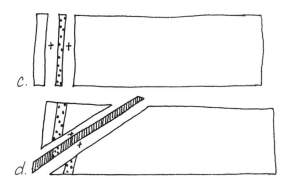

a.

b. ← CUT

c.

d.

Figure 3.27

TIPS ON PICK-UP STICKS

- Your design does not need to be preplanned. You can work across the yardage as you go. Use the finished cloth as regular yardage to make art-to-wear clothing (Figure 3.28), quilts, and other items.
- When you cut fabric on the diagonal, you are exposing the bias. Be careful not to distort the cloth when you resew the strips in place. Do not push or pull the cloth as you sew; let the feed dogs do the work. You can stay stitch the edges of the cut-apart cloth to reduce the threat of distortion.
- Note that the amount of space between the strips makes a difference. The empty space is equally as important as where you place the strips. Work the design on paper, narrowing, then widening the "white" space.

PICK-UP STICKS OPTIONS

- Use a printed cloth (geometrics, floral, etc.) for the yardage then cut through with strips of solid-colored cloth, picking up some of the colors in the print.
- Cut through with strips of hand-dyed fabrics in color gradations.
- Work in cottons or velvets. The effect would be striking. Just combine fabrics that require the same care (machine washing, hand washing or dry cleaning).
- Embellish the cloth even further by couching cords, ribbons, and/or threads across the yardage (see "Couching" in Chapter 4).
- Vary the width of the strips throughout the cloth.
- Use bold-colored fabric strips on soft-colored yardage to

Figure 3.28

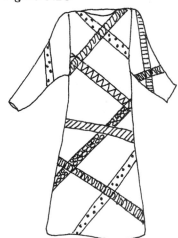

bring up the linear quality of the design. In contrast, muted strips play up the background cloth.

- For a different effect, lay the strips on top of the cloth and appliqué them in place.
- Liven the strip with patchwork—for example, a strip of triangles or different-colored squares.

MAKING A MOCK-UP

Anytime you can't quite visualize a design in your mind, you can make a more concrete example by creating a mock-up. This is a technique I used everyday when I was a commercial artist.

1. Use a proportional scale (available at art- or office-supply stores) to rescale your project. The proportional scale is made up of two concentric wheels of numbers and markers up to 90". It's easy to use.

2. Say you did a sketch of a pick-up sticks design. The strips measured 1¼" wide on the paper, but you wanted them to be 3¾" wide in cloth. You would set the inside wheel of the proportional scale at 1¼" and the outside wheel at 3¾". Look at the window on the small wheel. It says 300 at the marker, which shows the percent of original size. All of the rest of the measurements would be enlarged to 300%. Hold the two wheels in place to maintain the 300% mark and locate the next measurement off of your mock-up on the inner wheel. Across from it on the outer wheel will be the fabric measurement. A 4½" measurement on paper becomes 13½" in fabric; 3⅜" becomes 10¹⁄₁₆"; and so on.

STRIP QUILTING

Strip quilting is sometimes called "string" quilting. Essentially, lathes or slats of cloth are cut then resewn to form whole cloth. Many quilters prefer to use strips to recreate simple block shapes like the Log Cabin design. My personal interpretation is to piece strips then cut curved motifs. I appliqué these solid colored amorphous, sensual shapes to a richly patterned background cloth. I use more strips of sashing in various large florals to ring the inner block. See the "Awakening" denim jacket in the Color Section for a good example (Plate 9). Many books on the Log Cabin and other straight-edged designs are available (see the Bibliography). Here's how to work the undulating twist-and-turn shapes. Figure 3.29 shows the motif we'll use.

Figure 3.29

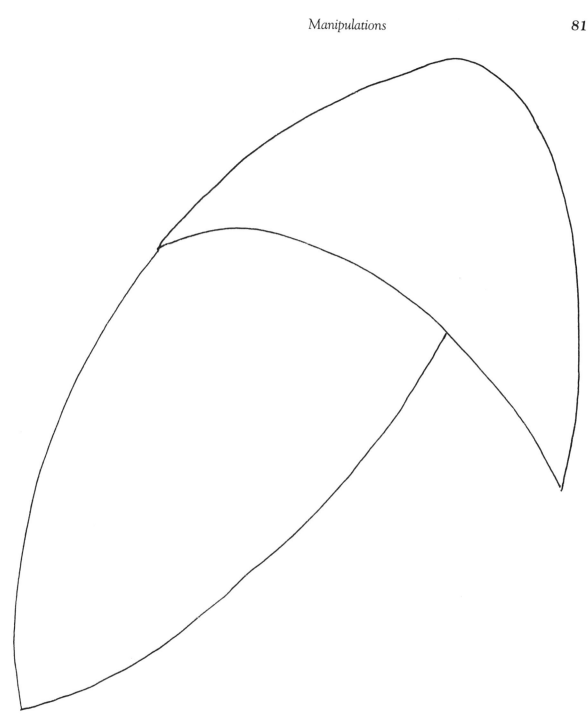

Figure 3.30

Figure 3.31

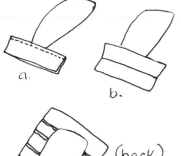

(back)
wrong side
facing

c.

trim off excess

Figure 3.32

1. Trace the design onto typing paper (Figure 3.30). Flip the motif and trace it again for the other side of the design. Cut each paper pattern into two shapes as shown in Figure 3.31. Seam allowances will be added when you cut the patterns out of fabric.
2. Trace the motifs onto a tightly woven cotton fabric. A loose fabric has the likelihood of warping out of shape as you sew. Baste the paper pattern to the back of the cloth, using long stitches around the outside edges.
3. Now select the fabric you want to use for the stripping. Any fabric will work. Cut fabric strips that are longer than the design shape. When the design is small in size, use strips of narrow widths; a large design can support strips of a more generous measurement. Consider proportion and try to visualize the final result.
4. Lay the first strip right side up on top of the cloth motif. Cover this strip with another strip, face down. Sew through all three layers and press the strip open (Figure 3.32a and b). Sew on a new strip. Open and press. Continue to the end of the section of one motif.
5. Turn the motif over and remove the paper (Figure 3.32c). Trim the strip quilting flush with the cloth motif. Press the seam allowances under and set aside.
6. Strip the other three design motifs (as in Steps #3 and #4). Finish as in Step #5.
7. Appliqué the motifs to a cloth or garment. Cut a circle (Figure 3.33) and appliqué it between the strip-quilted leaf motifs.

Figure 3.33

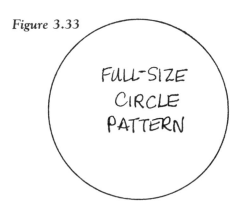

FULL-SIZE
CIRCLE
PATTERN

STRIP QUILTING TIPS

- Try strip quilting on simple shapes like squares and triangles.
- Vary the width, color, and texture of the strips.
- Turn the direction of the strips on the leaf tip to achieve the most effective contrast and definition (Figure 3.34).
- If you don't want to iron each added strip, use 100% cottons and "finger press" as firmly as possible so you don't end up with "pouchy" strips.
- Prewash all fabric before sewing.
- Combine fabrics that have similar care instructions.

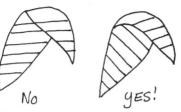

Figure 3.34

Quilting

Quilting lends an elegant embossed effect to cloth. Some areas appear elevated and smooth; the rest dimples into valleys, adding depth and dimension.

Quilting is currently enjoying a fevered revival. Many magazines and books are devoted solely to the subject, and quilting classes are being held all over the country. Art quilts are being shown in galleries. We love quilting!

Currently there are three types of quilters:

Traditionalists are those who work conventionally, using only 100% cotton cloth and historic patchwork patterns. The quilting is finely stitched in traditional heirloom designs.

Experimentalists may use traditional patchwork patterns but with new color combinations or different sets (positioning of the design). The quilting usually isn't as profuse or elaborate as that of the traditionalists. Sometimes it may be done by machine. The motifs may be designed by the quilter.

For **artists,** anything goes. Different fabrics may be combined in one piece. Paint and other artists' materials are frequently used. The quilting may be done by hand or machine or both. The patterns are free-form and the stitching is not as orthodox as the traditionalists or the experimentalists. Beads, buttons, and found objects may be attached to the quilt. And the quilt may be stretched on wooden bars as canvas is.

Within the different expressions of quilting are similarities as well. Some quilts, like the crazy, jump the boundaries. While crazies are considered a "traditional" quilt style, they occasionally are profusely embellished with beads, buttons, and charms. All quilters love the medium of cloth as a means of expressing themselves, and each can find admiration for the other's work.

THE BASICS OF QUILTING

The best way to learn how to quilt is to try it for yourself.

MATERIALS
Muslin
No. 10 or No. 12 quilting needle
Batting
Quilting hoop

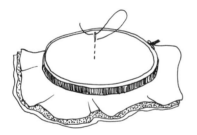

Figure 3.35

PROCEDURE
1. Place the batting between the two layers of muslin, making sure there are no wrinkles. Place the quilt "sandwich" in a quilting hoop (Figure 3.35). Tighten the screw almost all of the way. Check the fabric on both sides of the hoop and restraighten it if necessary. Tighten the screw firmly. Then push down on the fabric to ease the fabric slightly, so it isn't severely taut.
2. Thread the needle. If you have trouble threading such a small eye, use a needle threader, moisten the eye of the needle rather than the thread, and hold the needle up against a dark background (a sheet of paper or fabric) so you can see the opening easier. Knot the end of the thread. Bring the needle up through the bottom of the muslin and pull or lightly snap the thread so the knot ends up in the middle of the quilt sandwich (Figure 3.36).

Figure 3.36

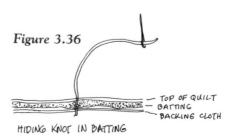

HIDING KNOT IN BATTING

3. Now hold the hoop so you will be stitching toward your body or to one side. Place one hand under the quilt hoop, then take three or more stitches on the needle by rocking it to pick up the cloth fibers. Be sure the stitches go through all of the layers of the quilt. The hand under the quilt hoop should be able to feel each stitch. Traditionalists are sticklers for the acceptable number of stitches per inch (16 being the finest, 12 adequate). I have heard stories of quilts with 20 stitches to the inch! In my opinion, the uniformity of the stitches are more important than the number of stitches per inch. You can always increase the number once you've mastered the technique. Try to maintain a uniform stitch length across the entire quilt or garment.

4. The step that seems to cause the most trouble and goes astray most often is reinserting the needle into the cloth. Try to gauge this maneuver so it is consistent with the rest of the quilting stitches. Before long it will become automatic and you won't need to think about it.

5. To finish a line of stitching, bring the thread to the back, take two small stitches, knot, bring the thread to the front, pull on the thread to hide the knot in the quilt sandwich, then clip the thread.

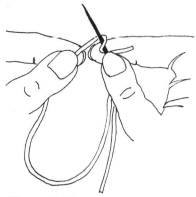

Figure 3.37

To give your handwork a finished look, try these tips for beginning and ending your sewing, taken from the milliner's trade.

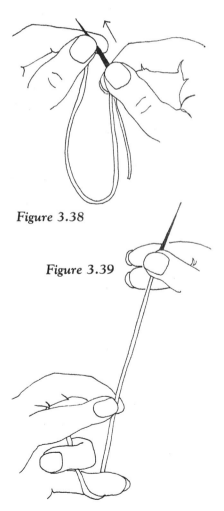

Figure 3.38

Figure 3.39

MILLINER'S BEGINNING

1. Thread the needle. Holding the opposite thread end between your thumb and forefinger, wrap the thread around the needle three or four times (Figure 3.37).

2. Carefully transfer the thread-wrapped needle between your thumb and forefinger to your other hand, holding the wraps secure (Figure 3.38).

3. Continue pulling the needle upward with the first hand while the other hand holds the knot in place, bringing the knot to the end of the thread (Figure 3.39).

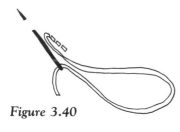

Figure 3.40

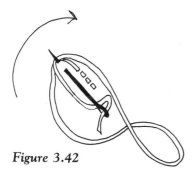

Figure 3.41

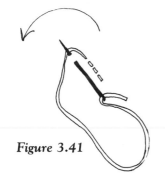

Figure 3.42

Figure 3.43

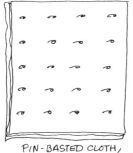

PIN-BASTED CLOTH,
BATTING, AND BACKING

1. Insert the needle into fabric, letting the point stick out (Figure 3.40).
2. Bring the right-hand side of the thread under the exposed tip of the needle (Figure 3.41).
3. Bring the left-hand side of the thread under the needle tip (Figure 3.42). Place a finger on needle tip and slowly push needle forward and out of the cloth.

QUILTING BY MACHINE

A "must have" for machine quilting is the even-feed foot. This sewing-machine foot ensures that all three layers will move along at the same pace. With a regular sewing foot the top layer moves along slightly ahead of the bottom layer, which is controlled by the feed dogs. Use either fine transparent thread on both the bobbin and thread spindle for a no-show look or use cotton thread to match the cloth. Adjust the stitch length to resemble hand quilting.

1. Place your machine next to your dining room table or other large work surface. This facilitates handling the size and bulk of a large quilt or garment. Otherwise, the sheer weight of the material will pull and distort the area you are sewing.
2. One of the major considerations facing beginning machine quilters is "How do I get this huge quilt under my sewing machine?" Once the quilt is safety-pin–basted every 6" to 8" (Figure 3.43), roll or fold the quilt from the sides inward (Figure 3.44). It is easiest to work the center first and keep moving outward toward the edges.
3. The most difficult section to work on (because of the bulk) is the center, so do it first. As your energy level drops, you will be working on the easier sections. Lay the quilt out

Figure 3.44

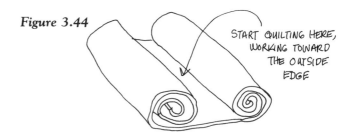

START QUILTING HERE,
WORKING TOWARD
THE OUTSIDE
EDGE

Plate 1

"Sissy Rose" Ultraleather suit. This snazzy suit is a good example of how embellishment can be used to highlight your face. A 6"-deep fringe cut from a strip of Ultraleather was inserted in the bottom yoke seam, and roses cut from a challis scarf were bonded with Wonder-Under, ironed in place, and then machine satin stitched onto the yoke. Gold cord was couched with invisible thread to add an accent. (See "Fringing" and "Appliqué" in Chapter 3 and "Couching" in Chapter 4.)

Plate 2

"Memory Bag." Display all of your treasures in this special bag with its see-through vinyl front. The bag is made in a tube shape; then the handle is made from a strip of cloth that creates the bag bottom, structural sides, and carrying strap. Instructions appear in Chapter 6.

Plate 3
"Marble Bag" hand tote. To make this simple but elegant bag I first marbled the fabric, then added the variegated crocheted rosette, which is embellished with a pewter button and coiled ribbon detail. (See "Marbling" in Chapter 2 and "Closures" in Chapter 4.)

Plate 4
"In Full Bloom" chintz vest (detail). This close-up view of the vest shown on the cover reveals how glitter paint and slick paint emphasize the preprinted flowers on the chintz. Shisha mirrors were attached with fabric cement and outlined with paint. (See "Painting Ho-Hum Cloth" and "Painting on Ready-to-Wear" in Chapter 2.)

Plate 5
"Wildflorist" cotton shirt. This clever shirt incorporates hand-dyed fabric, marbled fabric, and blueprinting done with ferns. (See "Marbling" and "Blueprinting and Brownprinting" in Chapter 2.)

Plate 6

"Flight Jacket." After the jacket pattern was cut out, lamé appliqués were bonded to the cloth and sewn in place. Then the jacket was layered for the slash and fray technique. Knit sleeves and trim provided the finishing touches. The detail shows the textured effect produced by slashing the sewn channels and exposing the layers of fabric. (See "Appliqué" and "Slashing and Fraying" in Chapter 3.)

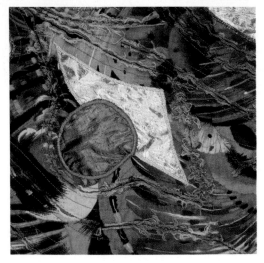

flat every so often and check for any folds or puckering. If you find any, restraighten the quilt sandwich and then proceed with the quilting.

4. Place the garment or quilt under the machine and begin quilting. If the quilting is rippling and your machine has this feature, decrease the pressure on the presser foot.

5. Whenever you can get away from premarking a design on the quilt or garment, do so. Use the quilting guide attachment (if you have one) to do echo quilting by going around the design elements. Or work in grids of squares, diamonds, or diagonals. As you quilt, smooth and reroll the material as necessary.

FREE-FORM MACHINE QUILTING

Another method of machine quilting is more useful if you prefer to do free-form, curved quilting designs.

1. Remove the regular foot and attach the darning spring (Figure 3.45). The spring only holds the cloth like a regular foot at the moment the needle enters the fabric. This allows you to move the fabric in any direction. It also prevents you from putting your fingers under the needle. Drop the feed dogs (optional). To practice, make a 14" quilt sandwich and center it on the bed of your sewing machine. Place your hands flat on the cloth with your thumbs almost touching one another (see Figure 3.45) so that the space between your hands forms a triangle. Your

Figure 3.45

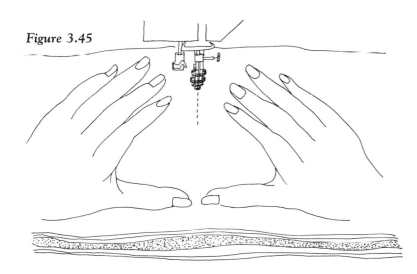

hands replace the feed dogs, and you can move the fabric in any direction: up, down, sideways, and in circles.

2. Always lower the presser foot lever and the top thread against the fabric. Then begin sewing by moving the quilt at a steady pace. In fact, the faster you can sew and still control the stitching, the better. You can see and feel when the movement is correct.

3. Practice on the sample quilt, traveling in all directions. To end a line of stitching, leave a thread tail. Use the tail to thread a needle, and bring the tail to the back of the quilt, take three small hand stitches, knot the thread, bring the needle to the right side, and bury the knot in the batting. Trim.

Figure 3.46 gives a sampling of quilting patterns in geometrics.

Figure 3.46

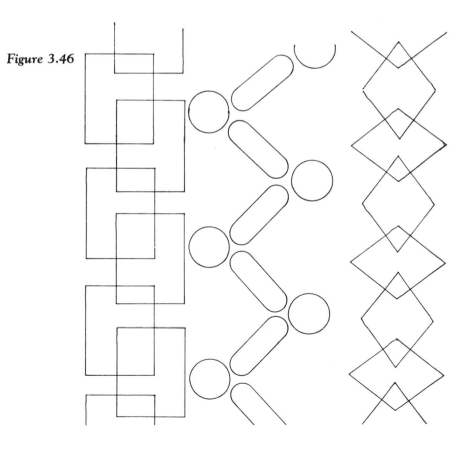

ITALIAN QUILTING

1. Baste two pieces of fabric together, wrong sides together.
2. Sew narrow channels from one end of the fabrics to the other.
3. Thread acrylic yarn on a rug needle and run it through the channels from the edge of the quilt or garment (Figure 3.47a). Watch for puckering. Ease extra yarn around the corners by using a pin to move the yarn into place (Figure 3.47b).
4. To finish, snip the yarn and sew closed invisibly with the satin stitch (Figure 3.47c).

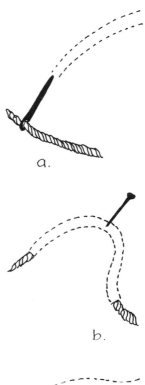

a.

ITALIAN QUILTING TIP

- To fill channels that don't reach the edge of the fabric (e.g., in a design in the center of a garment), cut tiny slits in the backing fabric and insert the yarn there.

b.

TRAPUNTO

1. Sew two layers of fabric together. You might want to use a printed floral with huge flowers. Sew completely around the motif (Figure 3.48a).
2. Turn the fabric over and make a small slit inside the motif. Using the eraser end of a pencil, stuff the motif with small bits of fiberfill (Figure 3.48b). Fill the corners first. Do not overstuff, or the motif will pucker. Stitch the opening closed.
3. Move to another area and continue slitting, stuffing, and sewing until complete (Figure 3.48c).

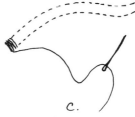

c.

Figure 3.47

Figure 3.48

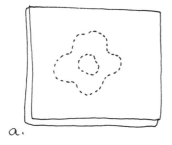

a.

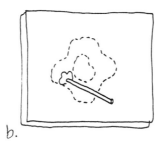

b.

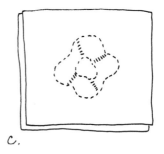

c.

MACHINE QUILTING TIPS

- If your sewing machine balks at using transparent thread on both the top and bottom, use transparent thread on the top and cotton on the bottom.
- If you want to mark quilting designs on the cloth, test the marking pencil for erasability before using it on an entire quilt or garment. If you use a temporary marking pen, test that it will wash out.
- Use the outline of a simple design as a quilting pattern. Trace the outline of a preprinted design (like a greeting card, for example). Quilting designs look best if they are kept simple, with minimal detail. Avoid intricate designs with picky little contours.
- Avoid any bulk in quilted garments by using muslin instead of batting.
- For quilting warm clothing, use a bonded batting or the new iron-on batting. Both will hold up well in items that will be laundered regularly.
- To better accentuate elaborate quilting, choose solid-colored cloth.

MACHINE QUILTING OPTIONS

- Use a flexible ruler to draw out unusual quilting designs. This snake can be manipulated into any curvy design.
- Look to nature for interesting quilting designs—a pine tree is a basic triangle with a small square at the bottom. A cherry is just a circle with a stem.
- Machine quilt using decorative machine stitches.
- Machine stitch on a bead or sequin every 6 or 8 stitches to enhance the quilting. Use beads with a hole large enough to accept the needle. Hold the bead or sequin in place with tweezers.
- Use the stitch-in-the-ditch method of quilting patchwork pieces; that is, quilt directly on the seam line of the patchwork. (Personally, I sew a fraction of an inch to the right or left of the seam line so I don't weaken the seam.)
- Quilt the garment upside down. Use a decorative thread, pearl cotton, ribbon floss, or embroidery thread hand wound on the bobbin (bypass the bobbin tension

and feed through the hole; increase the top tension) and use regular or transparent thread on the spindle. Technically, this is called machine embroidery, but many artists use this as a quilting technique.

Confetti Mosaics

I came upon this technique when I was designing the collar for the floral vest pictured on the cover. I wanted to create a collar that coordinated with the vest fabric yet had its own special appeal. The result is a collar made of tiny pieces of cloth fused between two layers of cloth. The top layer is transparent. I used organdy in this example, but you could use other sheer fabrics, like batiste or handkerchief linen.

Try confetti mosaics for collars, cuffs on blouses, the yokes of shirts, or a whole vest. The resulting cloth has a bit of stiffness similar to denim and wouldn't work well for clothing that needs drape, like skirts.

Here's how to do it.

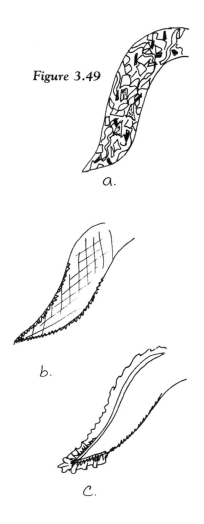

Figure 3.49

a.

b.

c.

CONFETTI MOSAIC COLLAR

1. Snip up pieces of fabric, ribbons, and threads. This is the confetti. Blend it all together by tossing it in the air to get a good mix. The fabrics you use for this technique will look more subtle in the finished piece, so use brights.

2. Snip up lots of small pieces of fusible web. The snippets are mixed with the fabric pieces to ensure everything stays in place.

3. Cut a top collar from white organdy. Cut a backing collar from white cotton fabric.

4. Lay the cotton collar face up. Sprinkle it with the confetti all the way to the outside edge (Figure 3.49a). Aim for even coverage. Cut a piece of paper-backed fusible web the same size as the collar. Fuse it over the cotton collar, sealing in the confetti. Remove the paper backing. Place the organdy collar on top and fuse all layers together. (Remember to protect your work surface from the fusibles!)

5. Use a serger to overcast the raw edges of the collar (Figure 3.49b). Sew lace onto the outside edge (Figure 3.49c). The inside edge will be sewn in the neck seam of the vest.

Figure 3.50

CONFETTI MOSAIC COLLAR OPTION

- You can also construct the collar by cutting another backing for the collar. Place the backing and the confetti collar together, right sides facing. Sew the pieces together around the outside edge. Trim close to the seam, then turn the collar right side out. Sew into the garment as usual.

The beauty of the confetti mosaic technique is that you can make your own colored, embellished cloth to match anything. Try it for handbags and other accessories.

Smocking, Pleats, and Tucks

Smocking, pleating, and tucks are all ways to gather and manipulate cloth to add texture (Figure 3.50).

Smocking

Smocking produces a honeycomb design. The easiest way to learn smocking is to work on a fabric like gingham. Because the gathering of smocking involves working on the four corners of a square, gingham, with its many squares, is smocked easily.

If you wish to use a solid-colored cloth you can purchase an iron-on dot transfer specifically made for smocking. Once you've mastered the technique you can work the smocking in a free-form manner as in the detail of the "Cake Dance" overblouse (Plate 10 in the Color Section).

Smocking uses up a considerable amount of fabric; buy three times the amount you'll need for the finished piece. Lightweight fabrics with a soft hand are most suitable.

BASIC SMOCKING PROCEDURE

1. Bring the thread up from the bottom on the first dot of the first row (Figure 3.51a).
2. Insert the needle in the next dot and slide it out immediately, catching just the dot (Figure 3.51b). Pull the cloth together.
3. Insert the needle through the same dot from the right-hand side once again (Figure 3.51c). This locks the stitch.

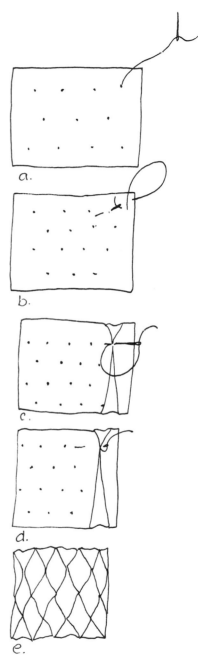

Figure 3.51

4. Insert the needle from the right and bring it up in the next dot (Figure 3.51d). Repeat to the end of the row.
5. In the next row, alternate with the dots you picked up in the first row to create the diamond honeycomb pattern (Figure 3.51e).

Smocking produces a stretchable fabric. My favorite way to smock is to use a feather stitch (rather than a running stitch) worked playfully across the cloth. I use a No. 8 sharp needle for smocking cottons and a No. 12 for fine, soft fabrics.

SMOCKING OPTIONS

- To create faux smocking, gather lines of stitching and then work across them with fancy machine stitches. Be warned that smocking done in this manner has no give, so measure accurately.
- Try using decorative machine-embroidery threads.
- Use one color of thread throughout the project for an elegant look; try a different thread for each smocking line to evoke a playful or ethnic approach.

Pleats

Pleats are made by inverting the fabric within itself. Traditional box pleats are folded inward on both sides (Figure 3.52). This pleat takes three times the amount of cloth stated on the pattern yardage chart on the back of the pattern package. Perhaps you remember the '50s pleated skirts made with two-color striped fabric . . . the skirt looked like a solid color until you walked and a different color was exposed. Very attractive! Chameleon skirts! If you would like to create one of these skirts, seek out cloth printed with wide stripes or create your own by sewing together strips of cloth. For box pleats, the inside folded section needs to be twice as wide as the exposed pleat. For example, if you want 1½″ pleats, the cloth would be sewn together in alternating strips of 2″ and 3½″. This allows for a ¼″ seam allowance to join the strips.

Knife pleats are skinny and folded to one side only (Fig-

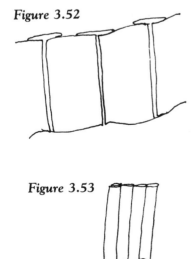

Figure 3.52

Figure 3.53

Figure 3.54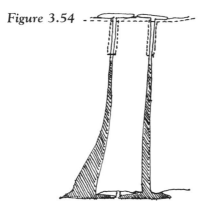

Figure 3.55

ure 3.53). For this type of pleat you will need twice the amount of cloth as needed for a "flat" skirt.

Press pleats and sew across the top edge to hold (Figure 3.54). If you like, you can sew the pleats down at the top for another look (Figure 3.55).

PLEATING OPTIONS

- Sew together a light and dark fabric.
- Use a solid color for the exposed pleat and gradated, hand-dyed strips for the inside.
- Use a solid color for the exposed pleat and a large-scale floral for the inside, perhaps a pictorial print.
- Use a large-scale plaid for the exposed pleat and a solid coordinating color in the interior.

Tucks

Tucks are made by folding the fabric under itself and sewing to hold. There are three basic steps: measuring, folding, and stitching. A ½" tuck takes up about 1" of fabric, so buy about twice as much fabric as you think you'll need for the finished garment.

Traditional tucks are made proportionately—both the top side and the under side of the fold are equal (Figure 3.56).

Blind tucks are worked close together and are usually quite thin (Figure 3.57).

Figure 3.56

traditional tucks

Figure 3.57

blind tucks

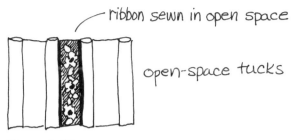

ribbon sewn in open space

open-space tucks

Figure 3.58

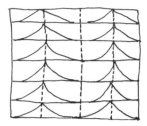

twisted tucks

Figure 3.59

Figure 3.60

pin tucks

Open-space tucks have a large exposed section and then a tuck (Figure 3.58). Quite often a ribbon or other decorative element is sewn down the wide exposed space.

Twisted tucks are made of a piece worked in traditional tucks that is further manipulated by sewing across the tucked piece against the fold of the tucks (Figure 3.59). You can either work in an equal-sectioned manner by attaching the quilting foot as a spacing guideline and sewing in straight lines, or you can work freely and run across the fabric in meandering lines. Use your fingers to push the tuck down in a reverse fashion as you sew.

Pin tucks are tiny raised ridges sewn with the aid of a special pintuck foot (Figure 3.60). They are usually worked in lightweight cotton or linen.

MAKING PINTUCKS

1. Insert a twin needle in your machine. Any sewing machine that can do a zigzag can use a twin needle. Add two spools of thread on the thread spindles, with the spools unwinding in different directions. Thread the needles. Attach the pintuck foot.
2. Mark the fabric and sew. The pintucks will automatically form. If you want higher ridges, tighten the top tension. Do as many rows of pintucks as you choose.

The tucking methods I've presented here are only a sampling of the possible manipulations.

TUCKING OPTIONS

- Try different folds and different ways to sew across the tucks to produce other variations.
- Try tucks in nontraditional fabrics like wool.
- Sew across the twisted tucks with machine-embroidery stitches.
- Think of new ways to use tucked sections as insets in clothing. How about sewing twisted tucked panels of black silk in a white silk blazer? Or using striped cloth to make the tucks, then twisting them to expose the other color?
- Although tucked panels are usually square or rectangular, why not try cutting them into diamond shapes or circles?
- If you are intrigued with luminous light, try working the tucks in a sheer fabric. The light plays beautifully through the layers.

Slashing and Fraying

If you look through books on historical costume (*Costume Patterns and Designs* by Max Tilke is an especially good book), you will find examples of slashing and fraying used centuries ago.

Today the slash-and-fray technique has been revived most notably by Tim Harding. His great coats, done entirely in this technique, are awe-inspiring. If you get a chance to see his work in person, go!

The basis of this procedure is to layer pieces of 100% cotton cloth; sew through all of the layers, making them one piece of thick cloth; then cut through the layers so the edges are exposed. You must use 100% cotton cloth to attain the frayed effect on the finished garment.

The number of layers is entirely up to you. Hypothetically, you could use only two layers of thin cotton fabric, but the effect would be skimpy. I would suggest at least four lay-

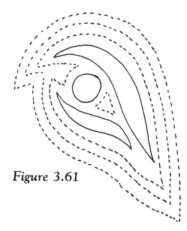

Figure 3.61

ers or as many as your sewing machine can comfortably sew through without balking.

In the example in Plate 6 of the Color Section I have used five layers of cloth. The top layer is a print, and all of the underlayers are solids that pick up some of the colors in the print. I did a lamé appliqué to echo the impression of the feathers flying in the air of the print fabric. I did echo quilting to emphasize the appliqué shapes (Figure 3.61). This is an excellent way to stress elements within a design. Here's a breakdown of the procedure.

SLASHING AND FRAYING PROCEDURE

1. Layer the cloth.
2. Baste all the layers together at 6" intervals using very long stitches (Figure 3.62). I do this by hand with strong quilting thread and leave long ends.

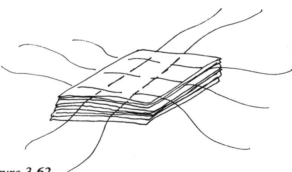

Figure 3.62

3. Sew all the layers together with your sewing machine. Some patterns you may want to try are illustrated in Figure 3.63: a simple grid, soft curves, a diagonal (or side slices), rectangles, and "lightning strikes." Sew through all the layers of cloth using a slightly elongated stitch length that has the appearance of quilting. Do not backstitch. Run the machine stitching across the entire width of the fabic.
4. Remove the basting stitches where possible.
5. Place the pattern pieces of the garment you wish to construct over the cloth (Figure 3.64a) and cut them out. Sew

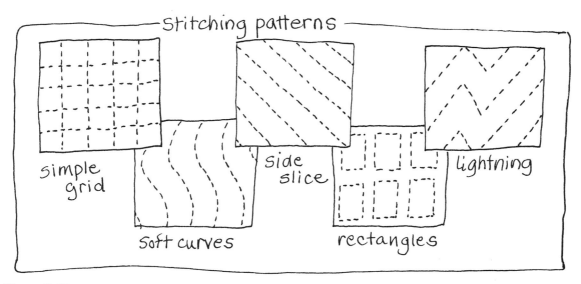

Figure 3.63

Figure 3.64

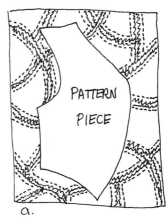

a.

around the outside edges of the pattern pieces about ½" from the edges (Figure 3.64b). This will add structure to the piece when you start slashing.

6. To slash, carefully cut between the quilted channels. Use very sharp scissors with *blunt* tips. You want to cut through the top layers, leaving the bottom intact. The bottom layer can be used as the lining. On my jackets, I made the channels wide enough to accommodate a particular pair of scissors. You may wish to manipulate the channels by pulling the back layer away from the others so you don't accidentally cut through it. Carefully slash the entire piece.

7. Sew the garment together as usual. You can expose the seams or not. The front edge can be left as is or can be covered with a bias binding.

8. Now comes the magic part. Wash and dry the garment twice. See how the edges fray and take on a ruffled appearance? That's the effect you are after. Now detail the garment by removing any stray threads. Each time you wash the garment it will continue to take on a marvelous texture. It will stop fraying once it has reached a stitching line.

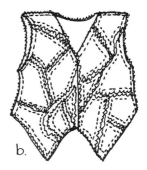

b.

SLASHING AND FRAYING OPTIONS

- Use a quilting stitch that echoes the design in a large-scale print on the top layer. Slash between the rows of quilting.
  Try using only solids.
- Use decorative threads for the quilting.
- Only slash part of the garment leaving some areas intact.
- Select different areas to expose different colors. Only cut through two layers in some sections, three or four in others.
- Use the slashed cloth as just a part of the garment. For example, do the bodice in slashing; the sleeves and collar in unmanipulated cloth.
- Stack solids on a picture print that will be exposed when the cloth is slashed.

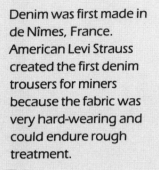

Denim was first made in de Nîmes, France. American Levi Strauss created the first denim trousers for miners because the fabric was very hard-wearing and could endure rough treatment.

FRAYED DENIM JACKET

This Frayed Denim Jacket is a great way to recycle denim jeans into a wonderful, everyday-wearable jacket. It goes with everything, has a great deal of style, and will garner you many compliments.

1. Grab a stack of used, well-worn jeans and cut out the least worn sections into equal-width strips (Figure 3.65).
2. Select an unconstructed jacket pattern (see Figure 1.21, in Chapter 1). Cut two linings from the same fabric. I used a brightly patterned polyflannel, but 100% cotton would be a good choice too. Place the lining pieces wrong sides together. You can baste them together if you choose, although I rarely baste or pin. Just keep the pieces in alignment as you construct the garment. You should now have two fronts, one back, and two sleeve pieces of double-thick fabric. Sew the shoulders together, then sew on the sleeves so the piece looks like Figure 3.66a.
3. The raw edges of the seams should be pressed open.
4. Now start to lay the denim strips in place. Piece the strips together if necessary to span the length of the fabric. I like to start with the longest area that needs to be covered, then fill in with shorter pieces on either side. Place the first strip on a diagonal across both jacket front pieces. Pin, then topstitch in place. Pin it across one front piece, across

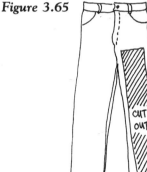

Figure 3.65

CUT OUT

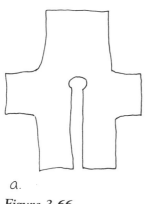 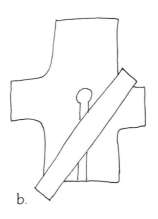 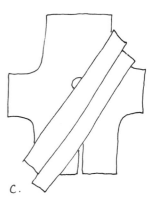

a.   b.   c.

Figure 3.66

the opening, and across the second front piece (Figure 3.66b). Sew in place. Abut second strip to first (Figure 3.66c). Pin it and then sew it in place. Continue adding strips until the whole jacket is covered.

5. Turn jacket over to the back and stitch around the entire perimeter. Trim off the excess strips (Figure 3.67).
6. Sew the jacket together with wrong sides facing. Backstitch at the beginning and ending of stitching lines (Figure 3.68). The neck edge, front, and hems are also left raw to fray.
7. Wash and dry the jacket to encourage fraying.

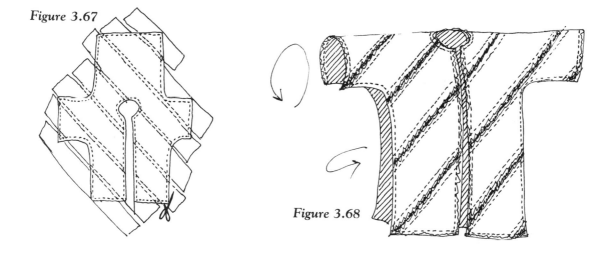

Figure 3.67

Figure 3.68

Weaving

Weavers entwine threads into lengths of fine cloth. I admire weaving in its pure form. It is such a powerful concept to take thread and create whole cloth. I imagine it must be the same sense of accomplishment I get from planting a seed in my garden and watching it grow.

In these pages I want to take the philosophy of weaving and translate it to the art-to-wear designer's palette. This is quite easy to accomplish with just a few adjustments. Instead of thread, use cloth strips torn with the grain, in any width you choose.

Instead of a traditional loom, use wooden stretcher bars (Figure 3.69). You can purchase the stretcher bars at almost any art-supply store. These bars come in many lengths, sized in 2″ increments (8″, 10″, 12″, 14″, all the way up to 48″) and you purchase them in pairs, with two sets needed to make a frame (two 10″ and two 14″ make up a 10″ × 14″ frame). The corners of the stretcher bars are united with a small wedge of wood that comes in the package. The size of the stretcher bars should exceed the length and width of your

"Wife" is a derivation of the word "weave." Single women in the early convents were called spinsters because they spun the thread with which the wives (weavers) wove the cloth. They rarely ever married.

Figure 3.69

a.

b.

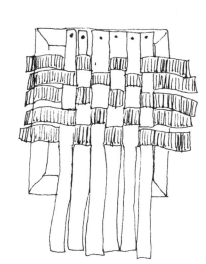

c.

project. It's always better to have a jot more than you need than too little.

If you are just sampling cloth weaving or wish to do a rather small piece, you can use a foam core board as your loom.

Whatever loom you choose, the method of weaving is the same. Remember weaving potholders on little plastic looms at day camp? I use the same technique, and it's just that easy, too. Our goal, however, is to produce a much more sophisticated design.

The first consideration is the cloth used for the weaving. Because the edges are exposed and not hidden in a seam, the type of cloth is an important feature. Either use nonfray materials like felt, melton, or the new synthetics that won't ravel at all; or serge the edges of the fabric strips before you weave. The other side of the fraction is to take advantage of the raveling abilities of cloth: 100% cotton produces a beautifully frayed edge, as does denim. Your choice of cloth will greatly affect the ultimate look of the woven piece. Each type of cloth will exude a different feeling. Try making up a few different samplers, if you have time.

CALCULATING YARDAGE FOR THE WARP AND THE WEFT

This process will tell you how much fabric you need to cover the loom.

1. Divide the width of the loom by the width of the cloth strips, then multiple by the length of the loom. This is the warp (vertical) figure.
2. To estimate the weft (horizontal) measurement, divide the length of the loom by the width of the fabric strip and multiply by the width of the loom.
3. Add these two figures together to find the total yardage of cloth strips.

Here's an example using a 10″ × 14″ loom and 2″ cloth strips: The warp is calculated by dividing 10″ by 2″, which equals 5″, and then multiplying 5″ by 14″ to arrive at 70″. The weft is calculated by dividing 14″ by 2″, which equals 7″, and then multiplying 7″ by 10″ to arrive at 70″.

Adding the warp (70″) to the weft (70″) brings the total amount of cloth needed to 140″. To convert this measurement into yards, divide it by 36″, which leads to 3 yards plus 32″ of cloth. I usually round *up* my yardage measurement to the nearest quarter-yard. In this case, I would estimate 4 yards.

BASIC WEAVING

1. To warp the loom, use push pins or staples to attach the fabric strips across the top edge of the wooden stretcher bar (Figure 3.69b). Abut the edges of the cloth strips so you don't have show-through on the final woven piece.
2. Beginning at either the top or the bottom, start weaving the crosswise pieces (Figure 3.69c). I don't pin or staple the weft. Again, abut the cloth strips as you continue to add to the weaving.
3. The basic tabby weave (the one used for those childhood potholders) is one over, one under. This is my favorite for use with cloth strips. You can achieve a great deal of variation in the tabby weave by using fabric strips of different widths and different colors. The example shown in Figure 3.70a is of just two colors. In Figure 3.70b, a variety of widths are used. And Figure 3.70c shows the effect of several patterned fabrics. More elaborate weaves can be accomplished with fabric strips, but it is necessary to cut the strips and resew them for correct placement. Figure 3.71 shows how to weave a heart motif.
4. Once the actual weaving process is completed, it is time to remove the piece from the loom. First pin the weaving at all intersections so that it doesn't shift when it is taken off the loom. If you have worked a tabby weave in wide (1½″ to 2″) strips, you may be able to remove the piece without too much pinning. It really depends on how you handle the cloth.
5. With your machine, sew across every other cloth strip, right down the center. Then repeat in the opposite direction.
6. Now the weaving can be cut to the size of your project. Try the piece as a yoke insert, sew it on patch pockets, make a jumper bib, or use smaller pieces in shoulder bags, totes, and fabric jewelry.

Figure 3.70

a.

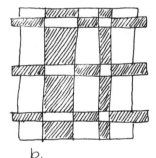

b.

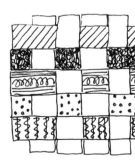

c.

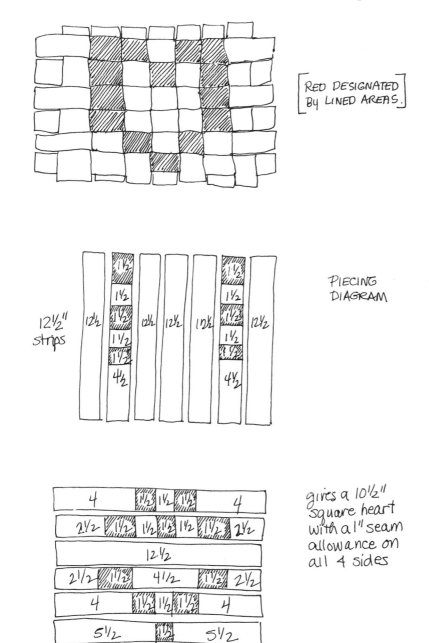

RED DESIGNATED
By LINED AREAS.

PIECING
DIAGRAM

gives a 10½"
square heart
with a 1" seam
allowance on
all 4 sides

Figure 3.71

WEAVING OPTIONS

- Incorporate heavy threads and yarns in with the cloth strips.
- Sew the strips together with decorative machine stitching.
- Try pinning the cloth strips to only one side of the loom; some people find it easier. Weave a strip and then realign the warp as you progress.
- Work out potential weaving ideas on graph paper.

Fringing

Fringing adds movement to a garment. Remember the flappers of the Roaring Twenties? The classic sheath dress was covered with row upon row of silky fringe—a little movement, and the dress shimmered. If you are interested in a "look at me" outfit, add fringe. It's always attention getting.

Whatever your attraction to fringe, be it practical or simply fun, add it for a jazzy look.

There are two types of fringe: self-fringe and applied fringe.

Self-fringe is made by removing the weft (crosswise, filler thread) from a piece of loosely woven cloth like linen (Figure 3.72).

Here is a great idea for adding interest to a simple dirndl skirt using self-fringe. Make up the skirt in linen or a linen-like fabric. Sew it together as usual, except leave the side seams open 10" from the bottom of the skirt (Figure 3.73a). Remove the weft threads from both panels for the entire 10" inches of the opening (Figure 3.73b). Gather the "strings" into evenly spaced bundles. Tie the bundles together by either (1) wrapping with the threads you have removed or (2) using an overhand knot (Figure 3.73c). Finish knotting all around the bottom of the skirt keeping the fringe knots evenly spaced and at the same level. Then make two more rows of knotted fringe by tying together pairs of bundles made from the previous row of knots (Figure 3.73d). Trim the ends of the fringe. This makes a kicky skirt you'll love to wear (Figure 3.73e).

Applied fringe—either made or store bought—is sewn onto the garment. Unless you are applying the fringe in a

> Native Americans used fringe on their garments for practical purposes. The "strings" of the fringe would shed rain away from the leather. Also, the swishy movement of the fringe shooed away flies and other bugs so prevalent on the prairie.

Figure 3.72

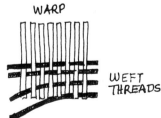

WARP

WEFT THREADS

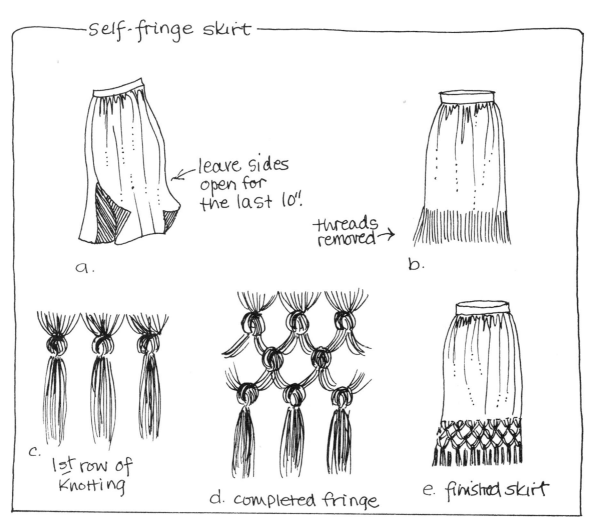

Figure 3.73

free-form manner, you'll need to mark the sewing line first with chalk or a washable marker. This will keep the fringe correctly positioned and give your garment a professional appearance.

I recently made a leather-look jacket out of one of the new microfiber fabrics. (Some machines have difficulty sewing on this fabric and will skip stitches. Neither my Bernina nor my Pfaff had any problems, but I solved this problem for a friend whose machine kept skipping by having her place a sheet of onionskin paper over the cloth and then sewing.) I wanted to use this New Age fabric to achieve a semi-traditional look. I made up the jacket, then added applied fringe across both the front and the back yokes (see the "Sissy Rose" jacket, Plate 1 in the Color Section).

To slice the 7″-wide length of fabric into ½″-wide fringe, I used the clever 6″-square ruler made by Omnigrid. (The ruler is printed in both white and yellow so it shows up on both light- and dark-colored cloth.) Using a small rotary cutter, I sliced the cloth every ½″, leaving 1″ at the top uncut. Be sure the cutter is very sharp for a project like this. If there is a blind spot on the cutting wheel and you need to go back over the cutting line it may destroy your fringe. You can use this method of cutting fringe on any no-fray fabric.

Another method of making applied fringe is to wind yarn.

WOUND FRINGE

1. Evenly wind decorative thread or yarn around a hairpin lace loom, which is available at sewing-supply stores (Figure 3.74a).
2. Cut a length of narrow ribbon. Mark a line down the center of the ribbon and lay the ribbon down the center of the wound thread or yarn. Place the whole thing under

Figure 3.74

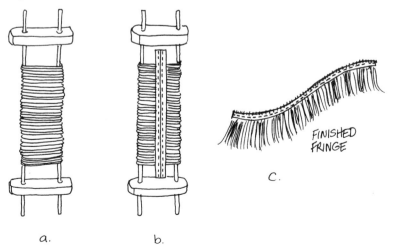

FINISHED FRINGE

a.   b.   c.

the machine's needle and sew a line of stitching on either side of the line marked on the ribbon (Figure 3.74b).

3. Remove the thread or yarn from the loom. Cut between the lines of stitching so you have two pieces of fringe. You can cut the fringe ends apart or leave them looped. Use the fringe on a garment by sewing a length of gimp or decorative braid over the ribbon to conceal the top edge or secret the raw edge in a pleat, fold, or seam.

FRINGING OPTIONS

- Add self-fringe to a denim sarong-style skirt.
- Sew fringe to the yoke of a cowboy shirt.
- Self-fringe the bottom of a wool tunic.
- Apply fringe to the under seam of the sleeves of a denim jacket.
- Sew fringe diagonally on a black silk straight skirt. Wear it with a sequined top.
- Combine different threads—metallics, pearl cottons, machine embroidery thread—in the wound fringe.

BRAID AND FRINGE EPAULET

Accent your shoulders with beaded epaulets!

1. Use satin rattail cord to weave the epaulet.
2. Start with a regular knot (Figure 3.75).
3. Pull Loops C and D down and twist as shown in Figure 3.76.

Figure 3.75

Figure 3.76

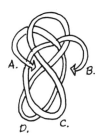

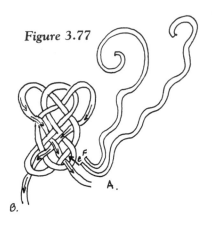

Figure 3.77

4. Lay twisted Loop C over Loop D. Weave the cord ends A and B, respectively, through Loops C and D. Pull gently into shape. Weave two more cords (E and F) through the braid, following the same weaving pattern (Figure 3.77). The pattern is easier to follow if you use cords of three different colors. Trim the ends (Figure 3.78) and glue a bead to the end of each cord.

5. Sew a braided epaulet to each of the shoulders of a ready-made shirt (Figure 3.79).

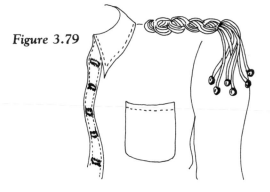

Figure 3.79

Figure 3.78

Adornments

Tassels

Moving from fringe (the last section in Chapter 3) to tassels is a natural progression. After all, a tassel is fringe wound into an adornment. A tassel has four parts: the heading, the wrap, the fringe, and the hanging cord (Figure 4.1).

Figure 4.1

A SIMPLE TASSEL

1. Cut a piece of felt into a 6″ × 12″ rectangle.
2. Cut the felt into ½″ fringe strips, leaving a 1″ header (Figure 4.2).

Figure 4.2

3. Apply glue to the header and roll up the felt. Secure the roll with rubber bands and let the piece dry thoroughly.
4. After the glue has dried, attach a hanging cord.
5. Sew a string of sequins around the header in a circular manner to finish the tassel off.

Another type of tassel is made from cords, threads, ribbons, or yarn.

A WOUND TASSEL

1. Cut a piece of cardboard 3" wide and as long as you want the finished tassel to be.
2. Wind the cord on the cardboard loom lengthwise until you reach the desired tassel width (Figure 4.3a). A full tassel looks opulent; don't skimp.

Figure 4.3

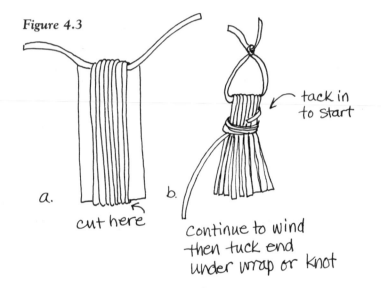

tack in to start

a.

cut here

b.

continue to wind then tuck end under wrap or knot

3. Insert a separate length of cord between the wrapped threads and the cardboard loom. Tie into a knot at the top of the cardboard. This holds the strands of cord together and becomes the hanging cord.
4. Cut the strands of cord at the bottom of the cardboard loom. The tassel is now free of the loom.
5. Use another length of cord to make the wrap. Wind the cord around and around the tassel near the uncut end, securing the ends under the wound section (Figure 4.3b). The wrap can be anywhere from one-quarter to one-half of the length from the top of the tassel.
6. Even up the tassel's ends if necessary.
7. Decorate the header, as desired. Figure 4.4 illustrates a few header ideas to get you started.

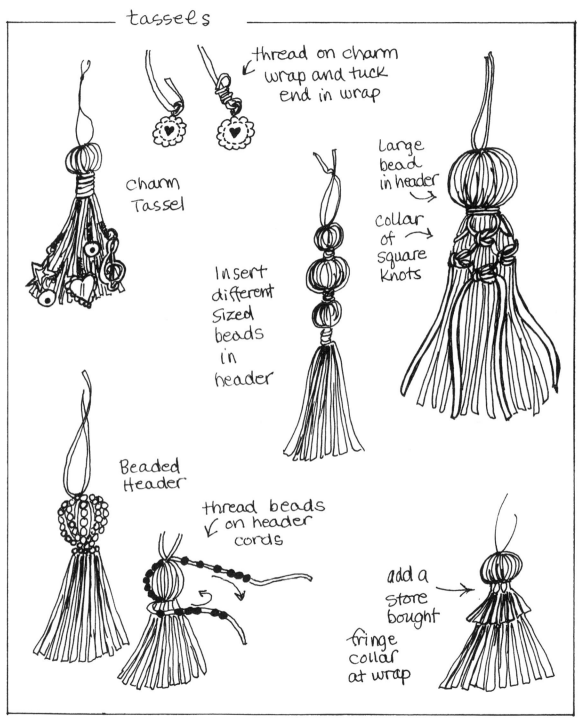

tassels

thread on charm
wrap and tuck
end in wrap

charm
Tassel

Insert
different
sized
beads
in
header

Large
bead
in header

collar
of
square
Knots

Beaded
Header

thread beads
on header
cords

add a
store
bought
fringe
collar
at wrap

Figure 4.4

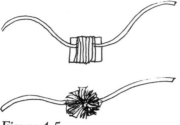

Figure 4.5

POM-POMS

Pom-poms, which are decorative balls of fringe, are a tassel variation.

1. To make pom-poms, make a generously strung tassel that is short in length.
2. Tie on the hanging cord (Figure 4.5) and remove the pom-pom from the loom and cut the loops apart. (A pom-pom does not have a wrap cord.)
3. Trim the ends evenly and fluff the fibers so they take on a ball shape.

TASSEL OPTIONS

- Coordinate your tassels to clothing made of linen or wool. Remove the threads from the cloth (see "Fringing" in Chapter 3) and create tassels to match.
- Try wrap threads that are a different type of fiber or a different color than the main threads of the tassel.
- Use a wide variety of threads and cords in one single tassel.
- Insert beads on the header cords before wrapping.
- Insert a large bead under the header cords before wrapping for a dimensional header.
- Ornament the ends of the tassel cords with beads, shells, miniature brass bells, or other trinkets.
- Bead the hanging cord.
- Braid the top layer of fringe.
- Check "Beading" (later in this chapter) and use some of those techniques to create an elaborate header.
- Add Fimo clay (see "Beading" and Resources) crowns to the top of the header.

Figure 4.6

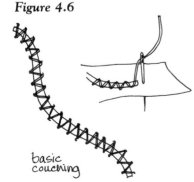

basic
couching

Couching

Couching, another age-old technique, is incredibly easy compared with more involved embroidery techniques. To couch is to lay threads, cords, or other fibers on top of whole cloth and then stitch across them to secure them (Figure 4.6). This is a good opportunity to use large-diameter threads that can't be wound on the bobbin or won't fit through the eye of the needle. Ribbons, rickrack, strings of sequins, and strands of faux pearls can be couched to cloth. Prewash any trims that may shrink. Ask your sales clerk if any special care is warranted.

Traditionally, many of the trims have had to be sewn on by hand. Now there is a glue and a special sewing machine foot made exclusively for adding adornments. The glue, called Fabric Tac, firmly holds any trim in place and will adhere during washing. The new couching foot (Figure 4.7) has a plastic attachment through which you feed the trim (two sizes are available). (See Resources for mail-order sources or ask your local dealer.) Using invisible thread on both top and bottom, you can sew across sequins!

Couching is a great technique to use on ready-to-wear, because you can add trims to any unlined garments and come up with a striking designer look.

There are two methods of couching: spontaneous couching (Figure 4.8) and pattern couching.

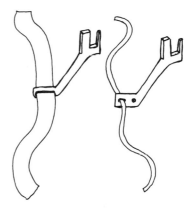

Figure 4.7

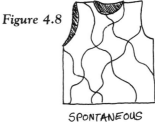

Figure 4.8

SPONTANEOUS COUCHING

SPONTANEOUS COUCHING

This effect is like free-form stitchery.

1. Set up your machine for a zigzag stitch that will just clear the width of the trim you wish to couch.
2. Place the garment and trim on the bed of the machine and lower the presser foot. Feed the trim through the plastic attachment on the couching foot or use an open-toed foot and hold the trim up slightly as you sew to facilitate the correct feeding of the trim.
3. Begin couching, turning the garment slowly to the right or left—it's up to you. Work back and forth over the cloth, applying the couched trim in whatever way you wish. Try to run the trims all the way to the end of the garment so the raw edges will fall in the seam allowance. On ready-to-wear, couch up to the hem and tie off the threads on the inside of the garment.

PATTERN COUCHING

With pattern couching you follow a predetermined design. Use either a gridded interlocking design or an outlined motif.

1. Set up your machine as described in "Spontaneous Couching." Using a washable marker, indicate the pattern on the garment.

2. Place the marked garment and trim on the sewing machine bed and sew the trim in place. Work the designs in order; for example, all the horizontals and then all the verticals. Gridded patterns work best if they run all the way to the edges of the garment. The raw edges will be disguised in the seam.

3. To finish off a couched design that ends on the face of a garment, leave long thread tails and decorative trim when you remove the garment from the machine. Thread the couching thread on a hand sewing machine, neaten and turn under the trim, and sew it in place with the couching thread. Bring the needle to the back of the cloth and tie off the thread. Sometimes when you are working with bulky materials, you may have to use an awl to make a hole to pass the threads through. Figure 4.9 illustrates four ideas to get you started with pattern couching: diamond grid, square grid, intersection, and Mondrian style. Try couching to echo a motif (Figure 4.10) or to outline a design or appliqué (Figure 4.11).

Figure 4.9

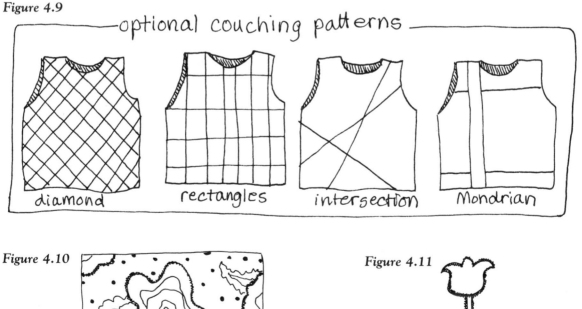

Figure 4.10

Figure 4.11

COUCHING OPTIONS

- Use a decorative machine stitch to couch.
- Lay a strand of pearl cotton over a ribbon, then couch.
- Couch two decorative armbands on the lower part of the sleeves of a blazer, as found on military uniforms.
- Couch two lines down the legs of sweatpants.
- Use invisible thread on top when you don't want the couching to show.
- Change the stitch width and length to see how it affects the final piece. Make up a sampler of stitching ideas.
- Make five or six rows of couched rickrack at the bottom of a full skirt, '50s style.
- Layer a bunch of different threads, then couch.
- Use a coordinating couching thread if you want the couched thread to look subtle.
- Try some of the new metallic threads—silver, gold, or variegated—or the esoteric rayons for couching.
- Hand couch using Victorian stitches like the feather stitch, blanket stitch, fly stitch, chevron stitch, or box stitch (Figure 4.12).

Figure 4.12

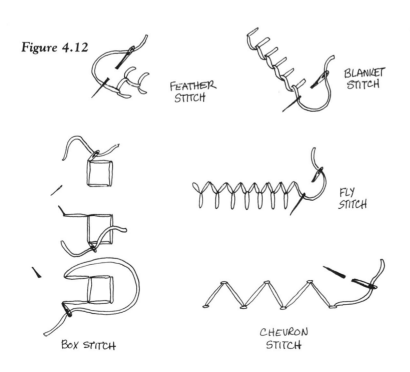

FEATHER STITCH

BLANKET STITCH

FLY STITCH

BOX STITCH

CHEVRON STITCH

Museum-Inspired Techniques

Some clothing I saw at the Elgin Public Museum in Elgin, Illinois, contained some great embellishing techniques.

Native American Thongwork

This technique graced the sleeves and lower front of a Native American tunic at the museum (Figure 4.13). Thongs of leather were woven in a simple looped design through the rawhide garment (Figure 4.14).

If leather is beyond your budget or desire, do the thongwork on another no-fray cloth, such as melton. Or try the technique with wired ribbon thread on any fabric ground.

Figure 4.13

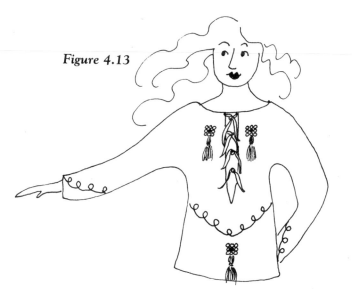

Figure 4.14

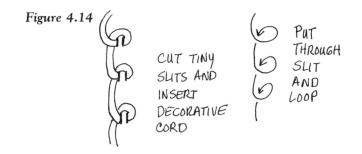

CUT TINY SLITS AND INSERT DECORATIVE CORD

PUT THROUGH SLIT AND LOOP

Beaded Flower

On the same tunic, beaded flowers were placed on either side of the centered neckline. To create these flowers, work three light-colored beads on the first line (Figure 4.15a); place one light, one dark, and one more light on the center thread; and finish with three light beads (Figure 4.15b).

Metals

On the stole of another tunic (Figure 4.16), flattened disks of metal, each with a large central hole, were attached at their top edges (Figure 4.17). You could substitute large brass or silver washers (available at hardware stores) for the disks. Sew them on using a satin stitch.

a.

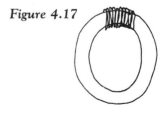

Figure 4.15   b.

Rosettes and Ribbon Tricks

Every once in a while I get in an utterly romantic mood and like to add dainties to garments, as our foremothers did to liven up their frocks.

I am enchanted with all of the possibilities of ribbon. Ribbon comes in infinite colors and widths. Shiny satin ribbons, ribbed grosgrain ribbons, wired ribbons, moiré ribbons, and ribbons with numerous motifs (hearts, geometrics, florals, and pictorials, for example).

The key word here is "play." Run a length of ribbon through your hands, then freely start looping it into bows and gentle knots. Get a book on how to tie seaman's knots and try them in ribbon. Take a look at some of the newer books on Japanese gift wrapping. The wrappings have such simplicity and elegance.

These two books are devoted solely to the subject of ribbonwork. *The Art and Craft of Ribbonwork* (see Bibliography) is a reprint of a 1921 booklet and shows many interesting examples of ribbonwork created by hand and by machine. Some of the pieces are quite elaborate. This book is well illustrated. *Old-Fashioned Ribbonwork* (see Bibliography) covers the the early decades of the twentieth century. It is well illustrated and offers many ideas for embellishing practically everything milady owns—even the lamp shades!

I'd like to share with you some of the ribbon tricks I learned from my mother and aunts. I suspect these are old techniques that have been passed down through the years.

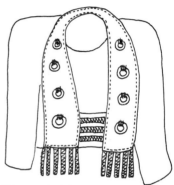

Figure 4.16

Figure 4.17

sew
ends
together
on back
side

Figure 4.18

When I create these ribbon manipulations, I work off of a spool of ribbon. The length of the piece you will need depends on how tightly you gather or work the zig-zags in the ribbon. Although I suggest specific widths of ribbon for some of these projects, in most cases any width will work.

Simple Rosette

Fold a 2"-wide satin ribbon in half lengthwise (Figure 4.18). Gather the edge and pull to form a rosette. Sew the ends together on the back. This makes a full, fluffy rosette. For a flatter rosette, do not fold the ribbon in half before gathering. Sew a bead in the center.

Chrysanthemum Rosette

Use ¼"- to ½"-wide grosgrain ribbon. Make a small loop on one end and stitch to hold (Figure 4.19). Make larger loops on either side of the center, as you would to make a bow. Turn the ribbon slightly with each loop so the loops don't lie on top of one another. Add however many loops you choose to create the desired fullness, tacking them to the center each time.

Petal Flower

Baste a zig-zag pattern across the ribbon (Figure 4.20). Use a smaller space on narrow ribbon, a broader space on wide ribbon. Pull the thread to make a five-petaled flower. Tack together with one stitch.

Cabbage Rose

To make a cabbage rose, begin as if you were making the Petal Flower, but don't gather it into a flower. Instead, make a longer piece with more zig-zags and roll the gathered ribbon. Take a stitch here and there to hold the gathers in place (Figure 4.21). You will need to stitch the cabbage rose

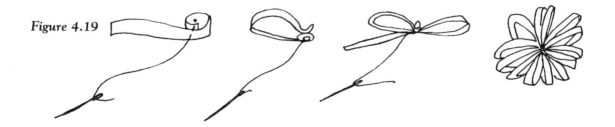

Figure 4.19

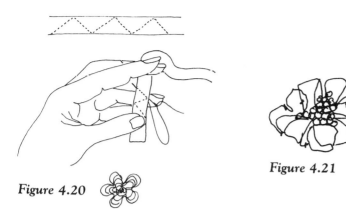

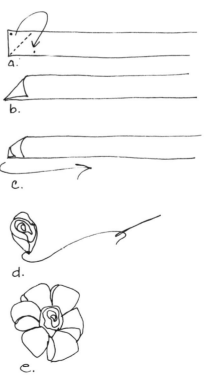

Figure 4.21

Figure 4.20

on a piece of interfacing or sew it directly in place on the garment. Sew a cluster of beads in the center.

Multipetaled Rose

To create a big, full flower, cut pieces of ribbon and gather each piece at the base (Figure 4.22). Use wider ribbons for the outside, then switch to progressively narrower ribbons as you make the inside petals. Sew all the petals together at the base.

Tea Rose

Start a tea rose by folding the corner of the ribbon flush with the bottom (Figures 4.23a and 4.23b). Fold the ribbon four times (Figure 4.23c). Glue or stitch the folds together (Figure 4.23d). For a rosebud, cut off at this stage, but for a tea rose do not cut yet. Gather the ribbon into loops around the ro-

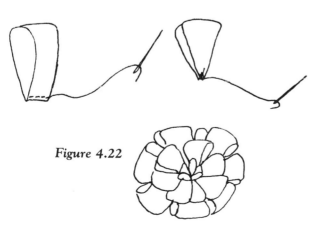

Figure 4.22

Figure 4.23

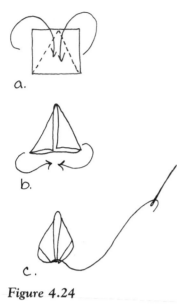

a.

b.

c.

Figure 4.24

sette (Figure 4.23e), then wind the ribbon around the diameter of the entire flower twice. Cut off the ribbon and sew the flower together at the base.

Leaf
To make a leaf, fold a piece of ribbon into a triangle as shown in Figure 4.24a. Fold the bottom corners inward (Figure 4.24b), but don't make a sharp crease, just a soft roll. Sew the bottom together (Figure 4.24c).

Simple Ruffle
To make this ruffle, baste and gather the ribbon along its top edge (Figure 4.25a). Try any type of ribbon for making ruffles. Stiffer ribbons will produce pronounced ruffles, soft ribbons a flatter, drapey ruffle.

Double Ruffle
The double ruffle takes three lines of stitching through the center of the ribbon (Figure 4.25b). Gather the ribbon.

Figure 4.25

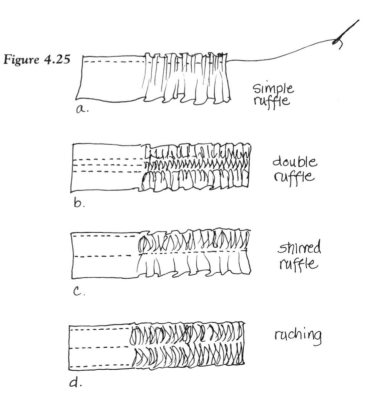

simple ruffle

a.

double ruffle

b.

shirred ruffle

c.

ruching

d.

Shirred Ruffle

Baste one line along the top edge of the ribbon and another line through the center to make this ruffle (Figure 4.25c) and then gather.

Ruching

To make ruching, baste one line of thread on the top edge, one in the center, and another on the bottom edge (Figure 4.25d). Gather the ribbon.

WOVEN RIBBON

MATERIALS

Long pins

Foam core board or flat Styrofoam in the size of your project

Ribbon (Try different sizes and types of ribbons for different effects.)

PROCEDURE

1. Pin warp ribbons in place along the top edge of the board.
2. Weave a weft ribbon across the warp (see "Weaving" in Chapter 3 for the basic process), pinning the ends of the ribbons in place (Figure 4.26). Continue adding the ribbons in the weaving.
3. Carefully remove the pins from the completed weaving and fuse the back of the piece with fusible interfacing. Now you can use the weaving in garments (Figure 4.27). Consider yokes in poet's shirts, inserts in pockets, handbags, and vests. What can you come up with?

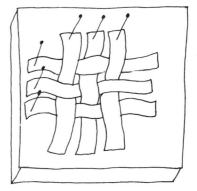

Figure 4.26

RIBBON OPTIONS

- Instead of gathering up the zig-zag ribbons into petal flowers, sew the zig-zag in metallics, gather them, but use them as lengths to embellish your clothing.
- Attach the flowers to barrettes.
- Glue ribbon flowers to shoe clips.
- Glue lots of rosettes and other ribbon flowers to a straw garden hat.
- Sew ribbon ruffles to a shirt you already own.
- Update a vest with ribbon ruching; bead the edges.
- Weave with ribbons of different widths and textures.

Figure 4.27

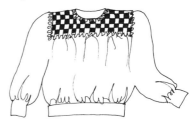

- Use a printed ribbon for the weft and a plain ribbon for the warp.
- Use woven ribbons for cuffs of shirts and bibs of jumpers.
- Weave in a diagonal direction. Appliqué to sweatshirts and jackets.
- As you work with flowers and ruffles, notice that you can achieve a great deal of variation by simply adjusting the amount of the gathering of the ribbons. Gather gently for a loose look; gather tightly for a crisp effect.

Beading

Beading adds action, motion, to a garment. A few beads added to a simple black dress glimmer beautifully at a subtly lit soiree.

I must confess I love beads. I've collected them for over 22 years. They come in many characters and moods, from tiny aurora borealis lined with sparkly metallic paint to big, chunky millefiore ("1,000 flowers") beads of fused glass or fragrant beads carved of sandalwood. Beads can be opaque, transparent, or iridescent and can be made of almost any material: glass, clay, porcelain, wood, bone, both precious and semiprecious gemstones, and metal. Figure 4.28 illustrates a

Figure 4.28

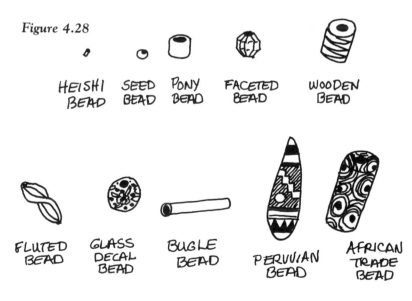

HEISHI BEAD   SEED BEAD   PONY BEAD   FACETED BEAD   WOODEN BEAD

FLUTED BEAD   GLASS DECAL BEAD   BUGLE BEAD   PERUVIAN BEAD   AFRICAN TRADE BEAD

sprinkling of what's available: heishi bead, seed bead, pony bead, faceted bead, wooden inlay bead, fluted bead, glass decal bead, bugle bead, Peruvian bead, and African trade bead.

Beads are sold either loose or in 12-strand hanks. It is also important to know that beads come in different grades. Be aware of this when you do price comparisons, especially in catalogs. Obviously, the grading is most important with the gemstone beads; the more nearly flawless, the better, especially when the beads are used at eye level (around the neck or on the top half of a garment).

Make Your Own Beads

Sculpey III and Fimo are two polymer clays that can be made into excellent beads. Both media are available at art- and crafts-supply stores or from the suppliers listed in the Resources section.

One-color beads are shaped to size, inserted on a thin metal skewer, placed across a baking pan, and baked at 270 degrees for 20 to 30 minutes (Figure 4.29).

To create marbled beads, take a piece of light-colored plastic clay and a smaller piece in a dark color. Work them together (not too much or the marbling will be lost and the clay ball will turn a solid color; the clays are mixable) and shape the mass into beads (Figure 4.30). Try a variety of shapes, not just the ubiquitous round. How about a square or a heart or a teardrop? Bake. The beads can be glazed with a matte or gloss medium.

Figure 4.29

Beading Techniques

When sewing beads to garments, remember to interface sheer and thin fabrics to support the beading. The more elaborate the beading, the more support needed. A sparsely beaded silk may need no support.

Here are the tools and materials you'll need:

No. 12 Quilting Needles. I use these for most of the beading I do. I like their thinness. Even tiny seed beads slip on easily, yet the needle has a substantial feel.

Bead Needles. This needle is ultrathin and quite long (around 3″). I like this one for beaded fringes and long lines of beading.

Quilting Thread. It is coated and easily threads into the

Figure 4.30

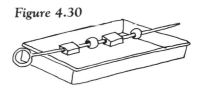

small-eyed needles. If you use uncoated threads, you may have to use a needle threader.

Lingerie Thread. I use this frequently on sheerer fabrics.

Beeswax. Run the threaded needle across the beeswax to keep both the needle and thread very smooth.

Sewing on Sequins with Seed Beads

First, bring the thread up from the bottom, then add the sequin, then the bead, and finally go back down into the sequin (Figure 4.31). Tie the thread off on the back of the garment.

Couching Prestrung Strands of Beads

Remove some beads from the string of beads so that the string can be threaded on a needle, brought to the back of the garment, and knotted (Figure 4.32). Thread the needle with transparent thread. Bring the needle up very close to the bead strand and couch over the string. Continue this process to the end of the strand. Tie off the thread on the back of the garment. Again, remove some beads from the end, thread the string onto a needle, bring it to the back of the garment, and tie it off. This is a good technique for making outlined shapes (Figure 4.33).

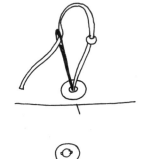

Figure 4.31

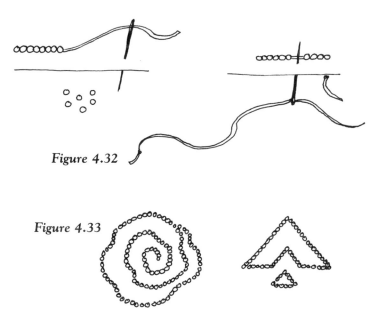

Figure 4.32

Figure 4.33

Figure 4.34

Figure 4.35

Figure 4.36

A Simple Dangle

Thread a needle and bring it through cloth. Add beads to the length desired, add a larger bead, then one smaller bead. Insert the needle back through the larger bead and through the row of smaller beads (Figure 4.34). Tie off the thread.

Cluster Dangles

Work three strands of simple dangles through a larger head bead (Figure 4.35).

Stepped Dangles

Work simple dangles in progressively longer lengths, then decrease back to shorter lengths. Continue along the length of the garment. The result is shown in Figure 4.36.

A Simple Edging

Start by taking two stitches in the fabric. Add small beads to the center of the drape and add a larger bead. Then string the same number of small beads on the other side. Take two stitches in the fabric and continue across garment (Figure 4.37).

EDGING OPTIONS

- Make a double layer, alternating the drapes (Figure 4.38).
- Drape and dangle the edging (Figure 4.39).
- Make a wrapped drape by working a second row around the first drape, perhaps in a different color (Figure 4.40).

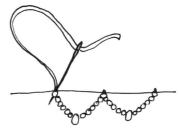

Figure 4.37

Figure 4.38

Figure 4.39

Figure 4.40

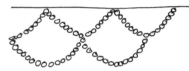

Figure 4.41

Two or More Layered Edgings

With a washable marker, mark across the fabric edge where the thread will connect to the cloth. Thread two needles and, with each of them, take a small stitch or two through the fabric. Place the needles together and add beads over both needles. Separate the needles (Figure 4.41). One needle will work the top tier; the other, the bottom drape. Take the top thread, add enough beads to reach the first mark on the the cloth, take two stitches in the cloth. Insert the needle back in the last bead, then add enough beads to reach the next mark on the fabric. Take the bottom needle and add enough beads to reach the center of the top drape or tier (Figure 4.42). Thread the string through the center bead. Continue across the garment. Tie the thread off when you reach the beginning of the beading. To finish off the bottom drape, feed the needle through the beads of the top drape and tie the thread off at the cloth.

Figure 4.42

LAYERED EDGING OPTIONS

- Make a double tier with a drop by adding a teardrop bead at the center of the top (Figure 4.43).
- Make a triple-tier drop by working with three needles (Figure 4.44).

Figure 4.43

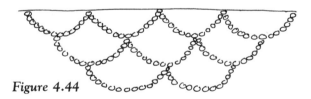

Figure 4.44

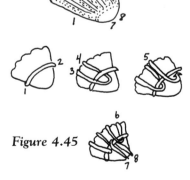

Figure 4.45

Attaching Shells

Use any medium-diameter cord (e.g., pearl cotton) rather than fine threads. Attach each flat scallop shell by sewing an anchor cord across the shell according to Figure 4.45. Come up at Point 1, down at Point 2, and up at Point 3. Loop the anchor cord and go down at Point 4 and up at Point 5. Loop the anchor cord and go down at Point 6 and up at Point 7. Loop the anchor cord between the other cords and go down at Point 8 and tie off the cord.

Dangles

To make shell dangles, you must drill a hole in each shell. Use a high-speed drill with a ¹⁄₁₆″ bit so the shells don't crack, and use medium-diameter cord for the dangle threads. Feed a length of cord through the drilled hole and bring up the cord about ½″ (Figure 4.46a). Then wrap it with another length of cord (Figure 4.46b). Finish off the dangle by sticking both cord ends under the wrap. Add a dab of glue.

Use shells on dress fronts, on the flap of a handbag, or on jacket lapels (Figure 4.47).

Figure 4.46

a.   b.

*B*uttons

Buttons are popular again. Buttons can radically change the complexion of a simple garment.

Although you can purchase a plethora of interesting buttons, some of the unique ones can be found at estate sales. I am particularly intrigued by pearl buttons—the larger the better. I usually sew them on upside down because I like the rough, multicolored side, especially on garments in natural colors such as browns, ecrus, and greens.

Pearl buttons, originally made from shells gathered from the Mississippi River, have quite a curious history. Early English street vendors became known as "pearlies" because they decorated their clothing with pearl buttons. As each peddlar tried to attract more attention, the pearlies' garments became more and more elaborate. Pearl buttons were sewn in intricate designs. The three garments shown in Figure 4.48 give a good representational feel of traditional pearlie outfits.

When I first heard about the pearlies, I found the idea of using clothing as a way to display a collection of pearl buttons appealing. So I made up a heavily embellished outfit. Then I realized how weighty these garments are. I would suggest either doing a small, heavily embellished piece, such as a belt, or using fewer strategically placed buttons on a garment to keep it more wearable (Figure 4.49).

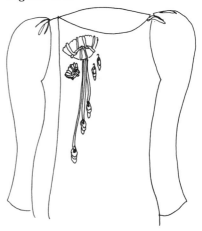

Figure 4.47

Buttons began replacing lacing in the fourteenth century. But the Puritans used only hooks and eyes, calling buttons "vanity." Certain groups, such as the Amish, still don't use buttons on their clothing.

Figure 4.48

Figure 4.49

Figure 4.50

BUTTON EXHIBITION NECKLACE

If you have a collection of pearl buttons or other curious buttons, especially if you don't have enough for a garment, you may want to make the necklace shown in Figure 4.50.

MATERIALS
Button collection of shank-style buttons
Crochet cotton
Crochet hook (size H, or whatever size works well for you)

PROCEDURE
1. Work a single crochet stitch for five stitches (Figure 4.51a). Insert the hook and pull up a loop, remove the hook and

poke the loop through the shank on one of the buttons (Figure 4.51b), reinsert the hook in the loop (Figure 4.51c), and make a stitch. Make five or more single crochet stitches in between each button. Note: The shanks on some buttons are large enough to insert the hook into. If so, there is no need to remove the hook.

2. Work the button exhibition necklace to the length you desire. Consider making a three- or five-strand necklace. The necklace should be long enough to fit over your head so you won't need a neck closure.

3. I finish the back with a large shanked button so I can tie off the five strands and conceal them under the large button.

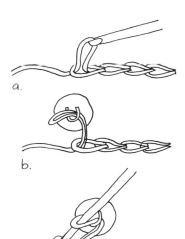

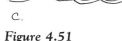

Figure 4.51

Besides pearl buttons, many, many other appealing buttons are available. Walk into any fabric store and you'll see rack upon rack of buttons. You can also buy handmade buttons from artisans at art shows. I've found buttons made of porcelain, ceramics, wood, even deer antler tips and polished bone.

You can also make your own buttons. Metal button blanks are readily available. You can cover them with the same fabric the garment is made of for a coordinated look. You can also work tiny embroideries on a cotton or tightly woven linen and use them on the button blanks. One caution: If the fabric you are using is not tightly woven, the metal button blank may show through the finished button. First prepare the button blank by painting it or back the cloth with a lining or fusible interfacing before attaching the button blank sections.

Polymer clays like Fimo and Sculpey III (see "Beading") can be used to create any kind of button you can imagine.

Knead the clays to make them malleable. Fimo is a bit stiffer, but it's better for fine detail. Fimo also is a jot stronger when baked. Slice off buttons with an X-Acto knife. Bake at 270 degrees for 20 to 30 minutes.

Circle Buttons

Roll the different colors of polymer clay into flat rectangles (Figure 4.52a). Roll the clay into a tube shape (Figure 4.52b). Wrap one of the flats around the tube (Figure 4.52c). Wrap another flat around the tube. Continue adding flats un-

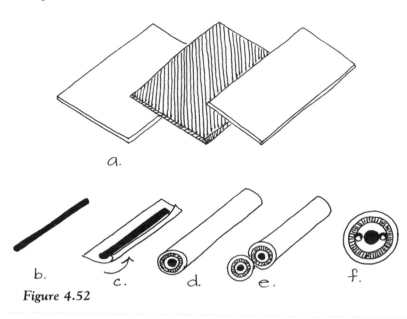

Figure 4.52

til the button is as large as you desire (Figure 4.52d). Slice the tube into buttons (Figure 4.52e). Make two or four holes in each button (Figure 4.52f) and bake.

Twist Buttons

Roll out two tubes of polymer clay, then wrap one tube around the other and slice (Figure 4.53). Make holes and bake.

Flower Buttons

Roll the polymer clay into one dark-colored tube, five light-colored tubes, and five medium-colored tubes (Figure 4.54). Roll out an additional dark-colored flat with a rolling pin. The dark-colored tube is the center of the flower. Alternate the light- and medium-colored tubes around the center. Then roll the dark flat around the whole thing. Slice, make holes, and bake.

Figure 4.53

Figure 4.54

Checkerboard Buttons

Roll out polymer clay of light and dark colors into squares (Figure 4.55). Place the tubes together firmly in alternating colors. Slice, make holes, and bake.

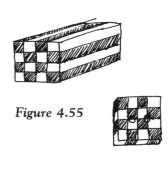

Figure 4.55

Extruder-produced Designs

You can purchase an extruder specifically made for polymer clay (Figure 4.56). It comes with 19 different discs. To use for buttons, roll out a tube and slice into buttons. Extrude some clay and place it on the button and bake. Glue the buttons to a button cover. The extruded clay can be used to create flower and checkerboard buttons, too.

Figure 4.56

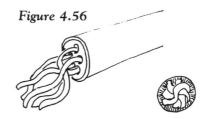

The polymers can be cut into shapes with tiny cookie cutters, too. Or you can hand shape the clays into anything you can imagine, including bananas, apples, moons, and stars (Figure 4.57). Either make holes in the buttons or glue them to a button cover. The best glue I have found for jewelry making and button attaching is 527 cement or a new silicone product called GOOP (available at crafts stores).

Speaking of button covers, if you haven't used them, they work like this: Click open the top, slide it over a button on a garment, and click closed (Figure 4.58). You can glue just about anything to the lids: silk roses, charms, thread tufts, a sprinkling of seed beads, plastic or china dishes from kids' sets, paper mementos, and coins.

Figure 4.57

Figure 4.58

Conceptual Art

Do you have an art-to-wear piece that needs a little something to spice it up? Toss a handful of buttons onto the garment and trace around each button and remove. Sew buttons in place corresponding to the tracings.

DECORATIVE WAYS TO SEW ON BUTTONS

- Try some of the knots shown in Figure 4.59.
- Liven up a tired old vest with a scattering of buttons (Figure 4.60). Tie them in place with decorative threads using a square knot. Either tie to the front and let the thread ends dangle or tie to the back for a more tailored look.

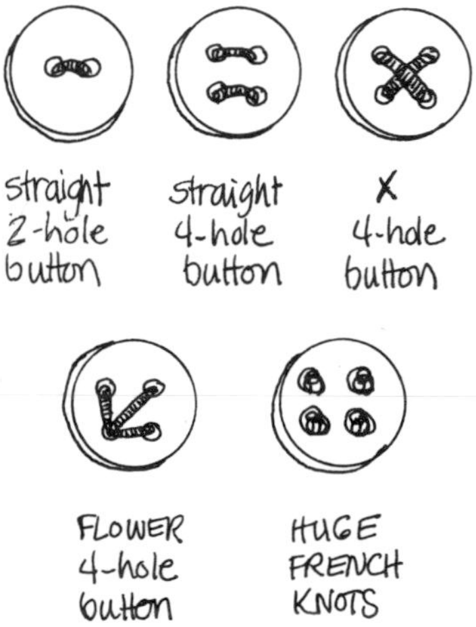

straight
2-hole
button

straight
4-hole
button

X
4-hole
button

FLOWER
4-hole
button

HUGE
FRENCH
KNOTS

Figure 4.59

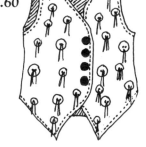

Figure 4.60

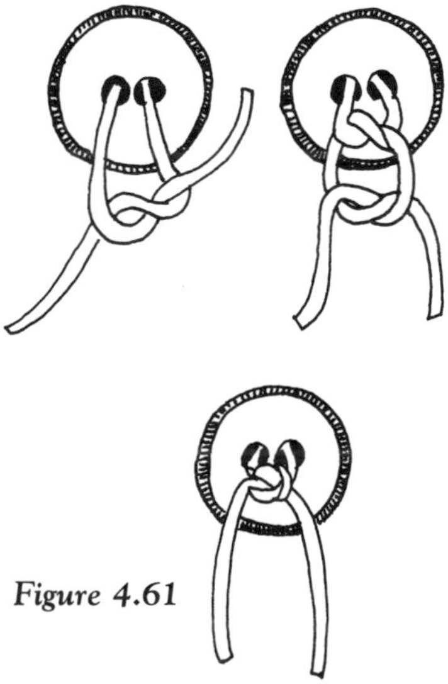

- To make a square knot, tie the left end over the right one and tighten. Then tie the right over the left end and tighten (Figure 4.61). This is a very secure knot.
- Use a wide variety of threads to create textural interest.
- Trace around the button on the cloth; remove the button. Work a chain stitch around outside edge of your marking in embroidery thread. Sew the button on as in Figure 4.62. Add Lazy Daisy stitches.
- Sew the button on following the diagram in Figure 4.63. Add French knots at the corners.
- For an asymmetrical approach, try sewing the button on as shown in Figure 4.64. Then continue the lines with quilting stitches in the area surrounding the button.

Figure 4.61

Plate 7

"Starlight" muslin jacket. The cloth for this jacket was hand painted with large brushes, then stenciled with silver stars and moons. Spontaneous machine quilting done with silver Madeira thread creates the fine detailing. (See "Stenciling" in Chapter 2 and "Quilting" in Chapter 3.)

Plate 8

"Fan Dance Neckpiece and Earrings." Very cleanly designed of paper-covered rectangles adorned with crisp pleats, this jewelry set is then further embellished with polka-dot beads. The set is an easy-to-make, sophisticated gift (instructions in Chapter 6). Why not present it in a special embellished box?

Plate 9

"Awakening" denim jacket. This pieced motif was appliquéd using floral fabric, then batted and quilted. The detail shows beading on the front of the jacket, which was done in a scalloped design with dangles. (See "Appliqué," "Patchwork," and "Quilting" in Chapter 3 and "Beading" in Chapter 4.)

Plate 10

"CakeDance" collage top. Silk, cottons, satins, taffeta, and other fancy fabrics were sewn in manipulated techniques (feather smocking, pleating, appliqué, etc.), then put together in a patchwork to create whole cloth. The top was cut from the cloth, and other embellishments like rosettes, beading, ribbon couching, and quilting were used to pull the random design together. Feather-stitch smocking is highlighted in the detail view. (See "Appliqué," "Quilting," and "Smocking, Pleats, and Tucks" in Chapter 3; "Couching," "Rosettes and Ribbon Tricks," and "Beading" in Chapter 4; and Chapter 5, Collage.)

Plate 11

"Chroma" melton big coat. Hand-dyed cotton designed in a striking V-shaped patchwork was appliquéd to form the strong lines of this coat. This is an excellent slimming design for the body. It makes the shoulders look broader, the mid-section narrower, and camouflages the rest. (See "Appliqué" and "Patchwork" in Chapter 3.)

Plate 12

"Peacock Feather Walker's Wallet." This slim bag is actually an oversized wallet that holds ID, four credit cards, a checkbook, a pen, and change. It's great for days when you don't want to carry a big purse. Instructions for the wallet are in Chapter 6.

Figure 4.62

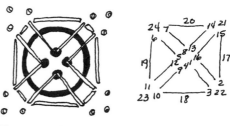

Figure 4.63

- Make button dangles by threading a stack of two-eye buttons onto two cords (Figure 4.65). Knot, add a bead, and knot again, letting the threads dangle. Sew the top cords to the cloth.
- Add a jump ring and a bell to one of the holes of a two-eye button. Knot thread through the other hole (Figure 4.66).

Figure 4.64

Closures

Just as buttons can dramatically change the appearance of any outfit, closures can either add or detract from a garment. The best way to select a closure is first to spend some time training your eye. Go to the finest clothing shops and see what big-name designers have used to enhance their lines. Often the simplest closures are the most effective in complementing the garment design. See what colors they put together. Keep a notebook of prize ideas.

Most of the techniques presented here are based on wrapping and knotting; others are "doodads" joking with the cloth, recycling found objects, and other innovations.

The first selection of closures are wrapped. You'll first need to concern yourself with the core. The core can consist of a single cord of any thickness or it can be made up of many strands of cord that you can break off into multiples when wrapping (Figure 4.67). Again, the center core can be

Figure 4.65   *Figure 4.66*

Figure 4.67   ← CORE CORD

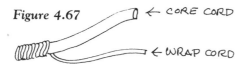

← WRAP CORD

1.

Figure 4.68

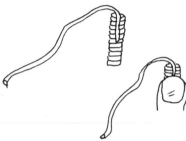

Figure 4.69   *2.*

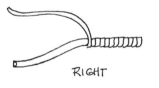

RIGHT

WRONG

Figure 4.70

anything from silk floss to heavy macramé cord. What becomes the core on one closure can be used as a wrap on another closure.

Beginning #1 (for fine cords)
Knot the end of wrap cord. With a threaded needle, stitch through the end of the core cord, pulling slightly to conceal the knot inside the cord. Begin wrapping (Figure 4.68).

Beginning #2 (for heavy cords)
Lay the end of the wrap cord on the core cord so each cord is going in a different direction as shown in Figure 4.69. With thumb holding the end cords in place begin wrapping. Wrap tightly so cord doesn't come loose.

Basic Procedure
Wrap evenly to cover core cord completely. Do not allow the wrap cord to build up on itself (Figure 4.70).

Ending #1
Thread the end of the wrapping cord in a needle and insert the needle under the wrapped cords (Figure 4.71). Pull the needle through the cords and cut off the excess so it is flush with the wrapping.

Ending #2
If the wrapping cord is too large to thread into a needle, simply trim the end short and tuck the excess under the wrapped cords (Figure 4.72).

Use Ending #1 for changing colors or threads on a closure. All beginnings and endings can be dabbed with Fray Check for extra security.

The following three wrapped closures offer three different wrapping techniques. The first one is wrapped then coiled, the second one is wrapped and coiled simultaneously, and the third one is wrapped in two separate sections and

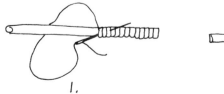

1.

Figure 4.71

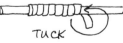

TUCK

2.

Figure 4.72

coiled only when worn or adjoining a garment. Each method uses a different cording system: The first method uses two simultaneous wrap cords, the second method changes cords for a color effect throughout the closure, and the third one employs a multiple-core cord.

Once you have completed the three closures you will know so many handy techniques that you will be able to explore unique examples of your own design.

DOUBLE-WRAP CLOSURE

The first closure is made of a soft cotton piping cord wrapped with black embroidery floss and turquoise Kanagawa (a rayon thread; see Resources). The decorative attachments are black shoe buttons I bought at an antiques shop (Figure 4.73). The button on the right covers the raw ends of the closure and the button on the left accepts the loop on the closure.

1. First, cut a 6" length of piping cord for the core. Tie the ends of three strands of the black embroidery floss together with the Kanagawa, leaving them attached to their respective spools. Attach the wrapping threads to the core using one of the beginning methods given earlier in this section. Wrap the wrapping threads over the entire length of the core cord. An interesting effect will occur; because the Kanagawa is much thinner than the embroidery floss, it will appear on the surface in a random fashion. End.

2. Coil the wrapped cord into Configuration A in Figure 4.74. Check that the loop will accept the button. You may need to loosen or tighten the loop to accommodate to the button you are using.

3. Sew the ends of the closure in place on garment. Sew on a button to cover the raw ends and another button on

Figure 4.73

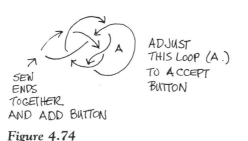

SEW ENDS TOGETHER AND ADD BUTTON

ADJUST THIS LOOP (A.) TO ACCEPT BUTTON

Figure 4.74

the other side of the garment's opening to correspond with the loop of the closure.

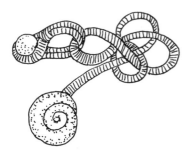

Figure 4.75

Figure 4.76

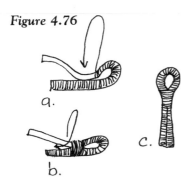

a.

b.

c.

SILK RAINBOW CLOSURE

This closure, which is featured on the front cover of this book, is done in six colors of silk floss (medium pink, ecru, leaf green, lavender, orangy yellow, and cyan blue). A pearl button is used for the closure and a pearl ammonium shell is used for the decorative attachment. It's quite striking (Figure 4.75).

1. Two sections are used for this closure. For the button section you'll need a 4½" piece of core cord. Beginning at one end of the core cord, wrap it with pink floss for ¾" and then end. Wrap with ecru for 2½", and stop. Fold the cord over to see if it will accept the button you will use (Figure 4.76a). Adjust as necessary by wrapping farther.

2. Once you have determined the loop size, wrap six times across both core cords (Figure 4.76b). Continue wrapping the unwrapped section of the core cord. Tie off and wrap with green floss for the last inch to finish (Figure 4.76c).

3. Sew the ends of the wrapped cord together and sew it in place on the garment. Sew the button on top of raw ends to cover them.

4. The second section of this closure is the coil. Cut a 14" piece of core cord. Begin with lavender, wrap for 1" and end. Next, begin with ecru, wrap for ⅜", and end. Begin with yellow, wrap for ¾", and end. Next use ecru again, wrap 2½", and end. Begin with green; to finish, gently fold the wrapped part of the closure on itself and wrap the green floss across both core cords. Continue with green for 2½" and end. Begin with blue and wrap for 2¾".

5. Coil the wrapped cord as in Figure 4.77 through Step d, ending with the cord behind the other wrapped cords. Hold the loops in place and wrap across all three core cords. Wrap the core with the blue for 1" more and end. Begin with ecru, wrap for 1", and end. Begin with yellow, wrap for 2⅛", and end.

6. Weave the wrapped cord through the coil in an under, over, under, over configuration. Glue a shell to the exposed end of the wrapped closure. Sew the coil to garment aligning with the button section of the closure. You'll

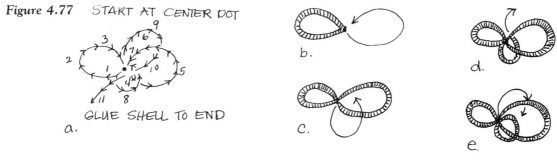

Figure 4.77   START AT CENTER DOT

a.   GLUE SHELL TO END

b.

c.

d.

e.

need to stitch it down only at the point where all the cords converge.

7. To close: Insert the end of the button section through the loop of the coil section. Bring the end of the button section back to the button and insert the button in the loop.

TIBETAN BELL CLOSURE

The final wrapped closure uses four strands of thin macramé cord for the core and is wrapped in a single color of pearl cotton. Tibetan bells are added for embellishment on the dangling ends of the closure (Figure 4.78).

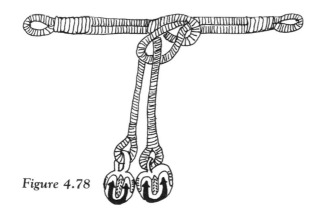

Figure 4.78

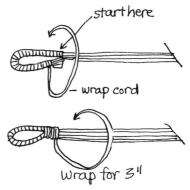

start here

wrap cord

wrap for 3"

Figure 4.79

1. Cut four 11" pieces of macramé cord for the left side of the closure. Lay all four pieces of cord together.
2. Begin wrapping 2½" from the ends of the cords (Figure 4.79). Wrap for 2". Fold back the wrapped cord to form a loop. Wind the wrapping thread across all eight cords for ½" (this finishes the loop).

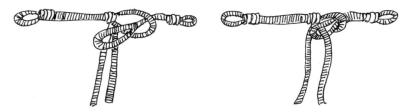

Figure 4.80

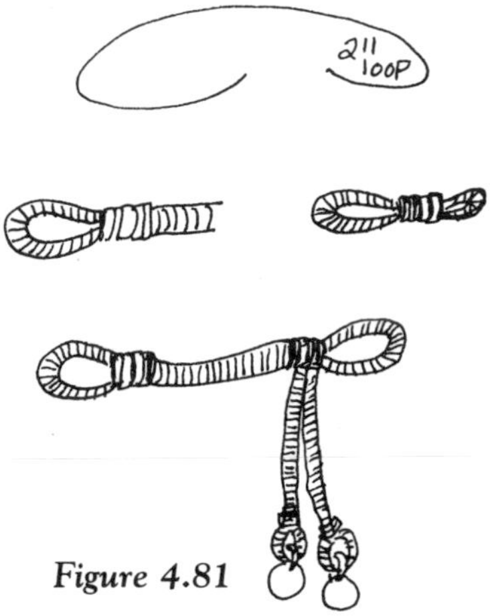

3. Now wrap the four cords for 3". Fold back ½" and wind around all eight cords to form another loop. Separate the hanging cords into two sets of two cords.
4. Wrap one of the sets of cords for 4" and add a bell (Figure 4.80). Fold wrapped cords back ½" to form a loop. Wrap across all eight cords. Trim off the excess core cords. Finish wrapping a few laps for a clean finish and cut off the wrap cord (Figure 4.81). Repeat for other dangle.
5. For the left side of the closure, cut four 7" pieces of macramé cord for the core. Wrap all four pieces at the same time for the entire length. Fold the cords so one end makes a 2" loop. Fold the other end to the same point. Wrap across all the cords to the end. Sew each closure section to the garment, attaching under the loop and wrap sections only.
6. To close, insert the loop on the left section through the loop on the right-hand section. Insert one of the dangles through the left-side loop to "lock" the closure (Figure 4.82).

2" loop

Figure 4.81

Figure 4.82

Doodads and Other Attachments

LATTICEWORK PLACKET CLOSURE

This closure looks great on patchwork jackets. The basic framework is constructed from bias strips sewn into a lattice configuration, leaving openings to accept buttons. This opening can be adjusted to any size button. As you can see in Figure 4.83, the lattice can be worked in a diagonal pattern or a horizontal and vertical one.

1. Cut whatever number of strips of bias you will need for the piece you are constructing. Work the measurements out on paper first if you want a close estimate.

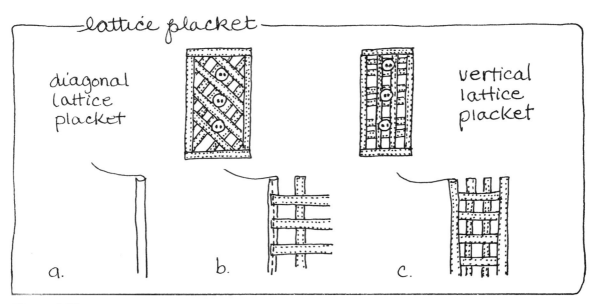

Figure 4.83

2. Pin the interior lattice strips into the configuration you chose and size the openings to the buttons you will be using. You can pin this to a grid drawn on graph paper if you want to keep the strips in perfect alignment. Topstitch the entire lattice. Remove the paper.

3. To attach the lattice to the jacket edge, first turn the jacket edge seam allowance to the top side and sew it closed (Figure 4.83a). Set the lattice on this edge and sew it to the jacket on the same stitching line (Figure 4.83b). Pin bias tape on top of this sewn edge and topstitch it in place (Figure 4.83c). To finish the other edge of the lattice, open a strip of bias tape, insert the edge of the lattice into it, and topstitch. Add the top and bottom lattice strips the same way. Sew the buttons to the other side of the garment, aligning them with the lattice openings.

A TWIST OF THE WRIST

The next closure was used on a velveteen cape. It's made of velveteen-covered self-cord worked into a simple knotting. (The first three steps describe how to make the self-cord.)

1. Cut a long strip of cloth to encompass a strip of cotton cord. It's better to use a strip that is too wide rather than a

strip that just fits the diameter. The excess will be trimmed away later.

2. Cut the cord twice as long as needed. With right sides together, wrap the cloth around the cord, starting in the middle of the cord (Figure 4.84). Attach a zipper foot so you can stitch as close to the cord as possible. Using a short stitch length, sew the cloth together; then stitch across the cord at the end near the middle of the cord. Trim very close.

Figure 4.84

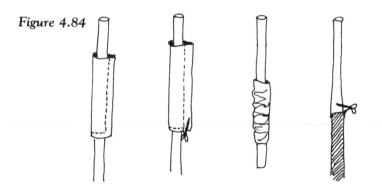

3. Now pulll the cloth down over the cord. See how the cloth covers the section of the cord where you didn't stitch? Cut off the excess cord and it's ready to use. You can cover self-cord with any fabric to match your garment.

4. To make the knotted closure, work the self-cord into the configuration shown in Figure 4.85. Pin the ends of the closure between the front cloth and the facing or lining of the garment. Sew the closure in place when topstitching the edge of the garment. Select a huge ornate antique button and sew it in place on the other edge of the garment.

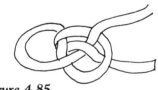

Figure 4.85

OVERHAND KNOTTED PLACKET

Another simple knotted closure is shown in Figure 4.86a.

1. Using two strands of satin rattail cord, make overhand knots at selected intervals (Figure 4.86b). Allow one side of the rattail cord to loop in an exaggerated fashion to accept the buttons you will be using (Figure 4.86c).

2. Couch the straight cord in place on the edge of the garment (see "Couching," earlier in this chapter). Conceal the raw cord ends in the finish of the garment (facing, bias strips, seams, etc.).
3. Sew the buttons on the other side of garment. I have used hand-painted porcelain buttons, which look marvelous. Dogwood Lane (see Resources) offers porcelain and ceramic button blanks that you can paint with acrylics and glaze. The button blanks come in different styles and can be exactly coordinated to your outfit.

The final doodad is an exercise in recycling. I made a small green-and-orange marbled clutch that needed a spicy closure (see Plate 3 in the Color Section). I found a small piece of variegated orange crochet at a garage sale and simply gathered it in the center to create a rosette. For further embellishment I added a pewter button and a braid of orange satin ribbon. When using the narrow ribbon, I noted that an interesting thing occurred: While the ribbon was being braided, I pulled on it and it coiled into a cord instead of just lying flat.

Play with the knots and recycle all the treasures at your fingertips.

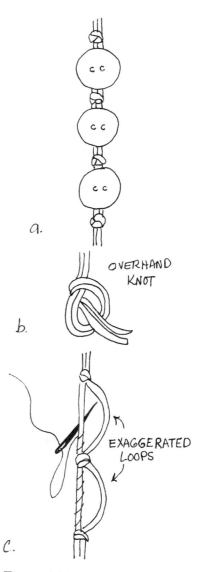

a.

OVERHAND KNOT

b.

EXAGGERATED LOOPS

c.

Figure 4.86

5

Collage
The Technique That Pulls It All Together

Collage is an artistic combination of disparate fragments combined together in one piece to create a unified composition.

This is a pull-out-the-stops, no-holds-barred technique! Here is your opportunity to display all of the samples you made in the Manipulations and Adornments chapters of this book on one smashing jacket.

I love a simple jacket embellished to the hilt. This pattern is one of my favorites—no darts, few seams—the essence of simple design (Figure 5.1).

OO-LA-LA JACKET

MATERIALS

3 yards base fabric (the fabric will show on both the front and inside of the jacket so choose carefully)

Thread

Fusible interfacing (paper-backed fusible interfacing (e.g., Wonder-Under)

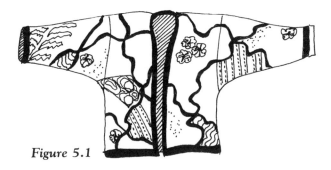

Figure 5.1

144

Beads, buttons, ribbons, and sample squares of the techniques
described in this book, such as patchwork, marbling, slashing and fraying, and others

PROCEDURE

1. Fold the fabric as shown in Figure 5.2. Measure from the
   neck to the shoulder, using the dimensions shown in Figure 5.3, and cut down the right-hand side. Measure from

Figure 5.2

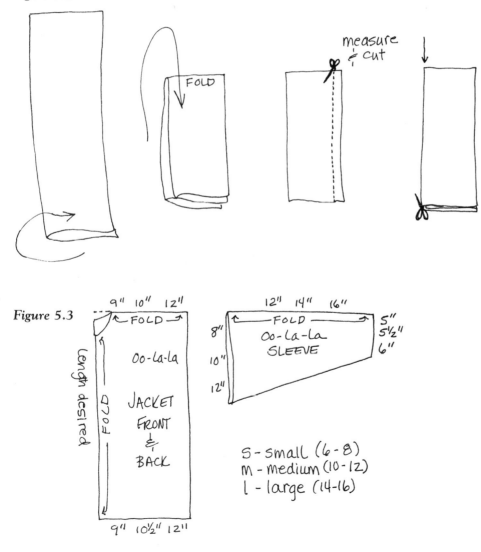

Figure 5.3

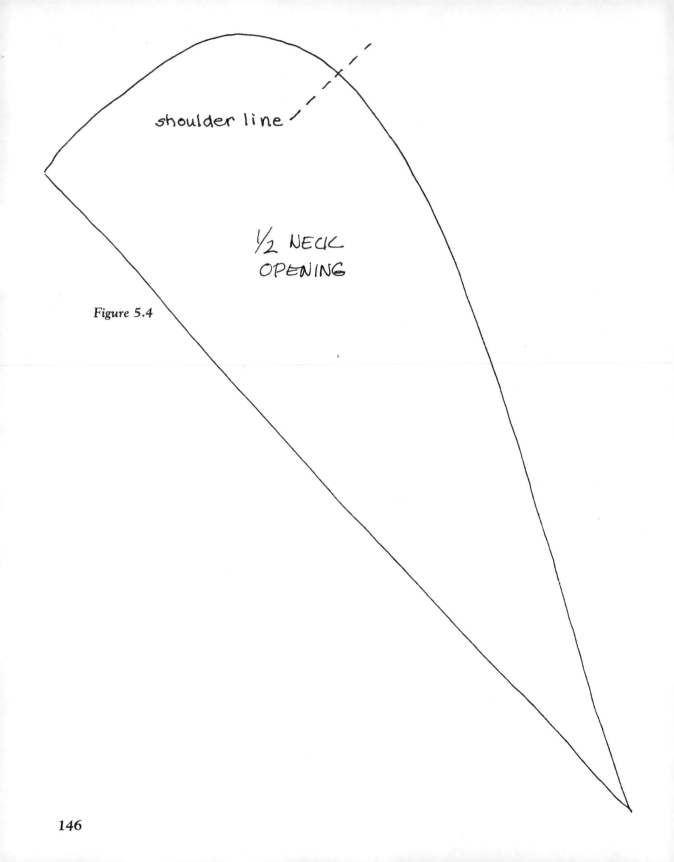

shoulder line

½ NECK
OPENING

Figure 5.4

the neck to the bottom and cut off the excess fabric at
bottom. (The jacket can be cut anywhere from waist
length to hip length. Use whatever length is the most
flattering to your figure.) Cut down the left-hand side, cutting only the outside layer of cloth; the inside is the jacket
back. This cut creates the jacket opening.

2. Open up the cloth. Use the neck opening pattern (Figure
   5.4) as a guide for cutting the neck. Trace the pattern and
   cut (Figure 5.5a).

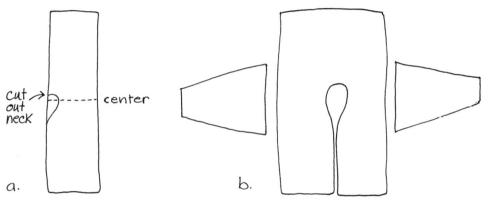

Figure 5.5

3. Use the remaining fabric to cut out two sleeves on the
   fold (Figure 5.3 includes the sleeve pattern).
4. Lay each piece out flat and start to plan how you would
   like to add all of your sample squares and embellishments
   into a cohesive design. Take time to study your grouping.
   Pin it to a wall. Lay it out where you can see it throughout
   the day. Change an element; look again. This looking part
   is essential for me. At any given moment I have pieces all
   over my house. I spend much more time looking than actually sewing. Once you like your arrangement, pin everything in place. Then, once again, look. Take the sleeve
   pieces and set them next to the main body piece of the
   jacket (Figure 5.5b). See if you like the way the piece will
   fit together. If not, rearrange to suit your artistic vision.
5. Begin sewing the elements on: appliqué by hand, use a
   decorative machine stitch, or couch with ornamental
   threads. Once the components are attached to the jacket

you may find that you don't like the separateness of the shapes. A good way to unite the design is to do spontaneous couching all over the jacket. Couch lines of ribbon or sequins. Or topstitch strands of pearl cotton.

6. To construct the jacket, working with right sides facing, fold the main body piece of the jacket at the shoulders. Take a sleeve, find the top center, and pin it to the shoulder of the main body piece (Figure 5.6). Sew in place and repeat for the other sleeve. With right sides facing, sew from the bottom of the sleeves, to the underarm and down to the jacket bottom. I place one pin at the underarm point to keep the fabric in place. Repeat for other side of jacket.

Figure 5.6

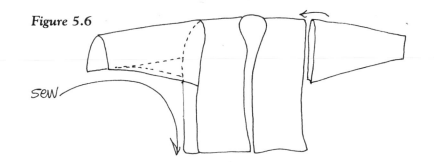

sew

7. Finish off the sleeves, the front, and the bottom edge of the jacket with seam binding. If you prefer a lining, cut a same-size jacket and add it, wrong sides facing, to the inside of the collage jacket before adding the binding.
8. As a final statement, you may wish to add more embellishment. Try some of the techniques you might have missed the first time through the book. How about spatter painting or beading?

Congratulations! You have just created a one-of-a-kind masterpiece. And, interestingly, if you are devoid of a good idea for a future project, just take a look at this jacket and a special, just-right technique may come to mind.

OO-LA-LA JACKET TIPS

- Place the most wonderful samples right up near your face.

- Place the least exciting samples below the armpit or on the underside of a sleeve. Try not to use beaded pieces in these areas; they may fall off easily when you wear the garment.
- If, when the jacket is completed, you find areas that need "punching up," appliqué on a design or do some extra stamping or stenciling.

OO-LA-LA JACKET OPTIONS

- Either sew the samples together, right sides facing, as in regular garment sewing or simply overlap the edges of samples and sew with a straight stitch. These seams can later be covered with ribbon or gimp.
- For a stained-glass effect, sew a solid-colored sashing between all of the samples to create a piece of whole cloth; then cut out your jacket.

6

Special Projects

This jewelry set, with its clean lines and pleated texturing, was inspired by art moderne and made up using intriguing pieces of wrapping paper (see Plate 8 in the Color Section).

MATERIALS

Mat board
Decorative paper
Felt, kid leather, or Ultrasuede scraps
Black satin rattail cord
2 shiny black beads with a hole large enough to accommodate the width of the rattail cord
3 large oval-shaped beads
Slick paint
White all-purpose glue

PROCEDURE

1. Use the patterns given in Figures 6.1a and 6.2a to trace and cut out one pendant base and two earring bases from mat board. Next use the patterns in Figures 6.1b and 6.2b to trace and cut one pendant covering and two earring coverings from decorative paper.
2. Glue the pendant base to the wrong side of the paper covering, centering the mat board within the paper. Fold the paper at the corners as shown in Figures 6.3a and 6.3b. This gives you a finely defined corner. Now fold in

PENDANT
BASE
CUT 1

a.

Figure 6.1

PENDANT
PAPER
PATTERN
CUT 1

b.

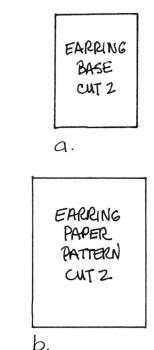

EARRING
BASE
CUT 2

a.

EARRING
PAPER
PATTERN
CUT 2

b.

Figure 6.2

each of the sides (Figure 6.3c) and glue them down. Set the piece aside to dry. Repeat the same procedure for the earring bases.

3. Using the base patterns, cut felt, leather, or Ultrasuede backings for the pendant and earrings. Glue the earring backings in place (Figure 6.4). Set aside pendant backing.

4. Cut a 30″ length of black satin rattail cord. Tie a bead on either side (use double knots on both sides of the bead 2″ from the end of the cord). Glue the ends of the cord to the back of the pendant (Figure 6.4) and let the glue dry. Glue on the backing and let it dry.

5. To make the pleated pieces for the pendant: Cut a piece of decorative paper 2″ × 3″. Pleat it in ¼″ sections (Figure

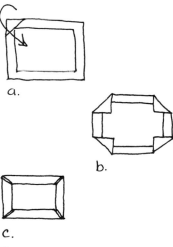

a.

b.

c.

Figure 6.3

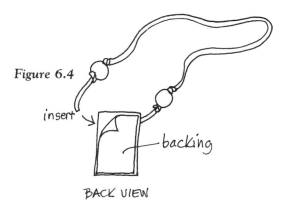

Figure 6.4

insert

backing

BACK VIEW

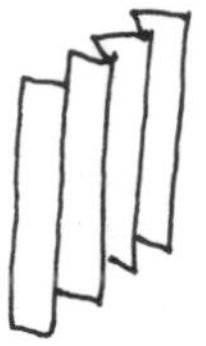

PLEAT AND PINCH
TOGETHER AT BOTTOM

Figure 6.5

6.5). Glue it onto the pendant. For the earrings: Use a piece of decorative paper 1¼" × 2½" for each earring and fold it into pleats as you did for the pendant. Glue the paper to the earring bases.

6. Glue the oval beads in place at the top of each pleat and decorate as desired with slick paint (I made polka-dots). Glue earring findings to the back of each earring ⅜" down from the top edge.

PROJECT OPTIONS

- Use fabric to match your garments. Cut fabric and place it on waxed paper. Coat the fabric on both sides with polymer medium and let it dry. Use the cloth instead of the paper to make the jewelry.
- Use different shapes for the bases (triangles, rectangles, etc.).
- Instead of one large oval bead as a decorative detail, use a cluster of small beads.
- Shorten the pleated sections for a perkier look.

M EMORY BAG

This is the perfect handbag/tote to show off some of your favorite things (as you can see in Plate 2 in the Color Section). The back of the bag wraps to the sides, which helps create sturdy double sides when the handles are added. The finished size of the bag is 9½" × 11½".

MATERIALS
Clear vinyl photo album page, 9¼" × 11"
½ yard no-wale corduroy, denim, or heavy broadcloth
½ yard lining fabric (this fabric will show through the clear vinyl photo page, so select carefully)
20" satin rattail cord
5 studs (optional)
Thread

PROCEDURE

1. Fill the photo page with mementos, photos, ticket stubs, stickers, flat buttons, decorative threads, and trinkets; use

anything flat that has meaning for you. Once the page is filled to your satisfaction, sew across the top edge of the bottom three pockets so debris from the bag doesn't enter the vinyl pockets (Figure 6.6). You can leave it open if you wish to change the memento collection, but you'll need to keep a tidy bag.

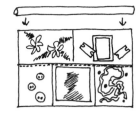

Figure 6.6

2. Cut a fabric strip 2½″ × 12″. Fold the raw edges to the inside. Sew this binding strip along the top edge of the album page (Figure 6.6). Trim away the excess fabric at the ends.

3. Cut two panels 10¼″ × 16″, one each from the bag and lining fabrics. Place the two pieces together, right sides facing. Using a ½″ seam allowance, sew them together, leaving a 4″ opening for turning (Figure 6.7). Trim the seams and corners and turn right side out (Figure 6.8). Finger press.

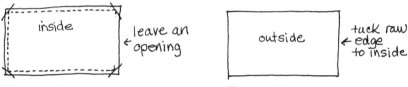

Figure 6.7   **Figure 6.8**

4. Place the photo page and the bag fabric right sides together and sew along both side seams, using a ¼″ seam allowance (Figure 6.9). Do not place pins in the vinyl, or you will have permanent holes. Instead, line up the edges flush and hold them with your fingers as you feed the material through the machine. Do not turn the bag right side out at this point.

Figure 6.9

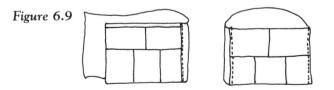

5. Cut a piece of bag fabric 4″ × 45″ for the sides, bottom, and handle. Fold the cloth in half lengthwise, right sides together, and sew along the long edge. Turn right side

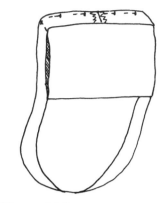

Figure 6.10

out. Line up the short sides and sew together. Center this seam on the bottom of the bag and line up with the bottom edges of the fabric back and photo vinyl front (Figure 6.10). To complete the bottom of the bag, sew the strip to the back and front of the bag, but do not sew the corner (Figure 6.11). Carefully turn the bag right side out, using your fingers to push out the inside corners and shape the bag. Line the fabric strip up with the sides of the front and back pieces (Figure 6.12). From the inside of the bag, whipstitch the fabric strip (sides) to the bag at the top and bottom of the bag on both sides.

Figure 6.11

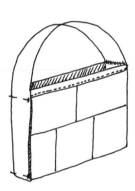

Figure 6.12

6. Find the center of the bag's handle. Then find the center of the rattail cord and place it on the handle. Wrap the cord in place (Figure 6.13). (See the beginnings and endings in "Closures" in Chapter 4.) Tuck the ends of the cord under the wound section and glue in place. Your bag is now complete (Figure 6.14).

Figure 6.13

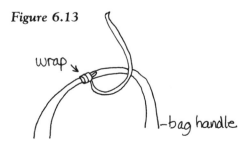

wrap

—bag handle

Figure 6.14

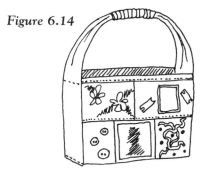

PEACOCK FEATHER WALKER'S WALLET

This is a slimline, lightweight bag to throw over your shoulder for a day of shopping or touring (Color Plate 12). The wallet opens flat to reveal an inside that is fully compartmentalized to hold the essentials. The decorative detail on the face of the bag is elegant enough for a fancy celebration (Figure 6.15). The finished oversized wallet measures 6" × 9" when closed.

MATERIALS
½ yard Black pima cotton
5½" × 8" piece of gold lamé
Peacock feather
Two pieces of clear vinyl, 5½" × 8" and 2½" × 4" (available at
    hardware stores)
Paper-backed fusible web (Wonder-Under)

Figure 6.15

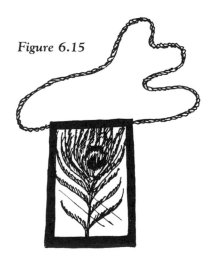

¼ yard Ultraleather
10" piece of Velcro, black, ¾" wide
Black thread
1 yard black cord

PROCEDURE

Figure 6.16 shows a schematic view of the inside of the bag. Take a look at the placement of the pockets now; then refer back to the figure as you sew to clarify anything you can't visualize.

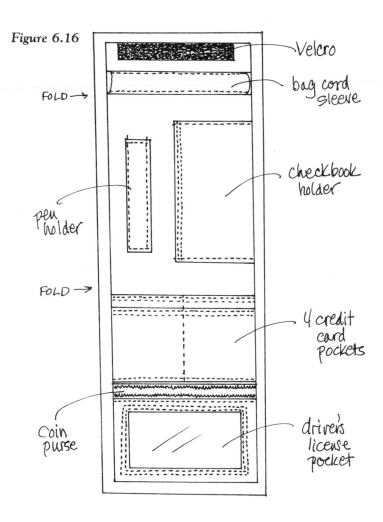

Figure 6.16

FOLD →

FOLD →

FOLD →

Velcro

bag cord sleeve

checkbook holder

pen holder

4 credit card pockets

Coin purse

driver's license pocket

1. Cut two pieces of black cotton 5½" × 20". Set one aside for the inside of the bag. Use the other piece for the outside of the bag.

2. Cut a strip of Velcro 4½". Pull the Velcro apart. Measure ¾" up from the short end of the black cotton panel, center, and sew the loop section of the Velcro in place (Figure 6.17).

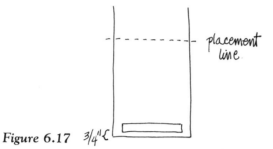

Figure 6.17

3. Measure and mark 8½" up from the Velcro end of the black cotton panel. This is the placement line for the peacock feather decoration.

4. Fuse the lamé to the Wonder-Under, following the directions on the package. Fuse the backed lamé to a piece of black cotton and trim to 5½" × 8". Lay the peacock feather on the lamé and cover with the 5½" × 8" vinyl piece.

5. Cut two strips of Ultraleather 1" × 5½". Turn the long sides under ½". Place one of the leather strips at the bottom of the vinyl/feather/lamé piece and edgestitch (Figure 6.18). Repeat for the top of the decorative panel.

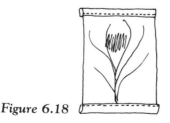

Figure 6.18

6. Now place the bottom edge of the decorative panel on the placement line you marked on the black cotton panel in Step #3. Edgestitch across the Ultraleather binding to

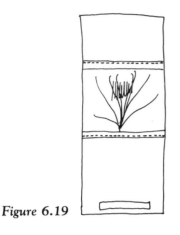

Figure 6.19

connect the decorative panel to the black cotton panel
(Figure 6.19). You've created the outside of the bag. Set it
aside.

7. Use black cotton cloth for all of the pockets. Using pattern
given in Figure 6.20, cut out the driver's license pocket.
Turn the top edge under ¼" twice. Edgestitch the top
edge; then sew another line of stitching ⅜" down from
the first (Figure 6.21).

8. Cut out center window. Clip to the corners and finger
press the cloth to the inside (Figure 6.21). Center the 2½"
× 4" piece of vinyl behind the cut-out window in the
cloth. Edgestitch the vinyl in place and sew around again
⅛" from the first line (Figure 6.22). Set aside.

9. Cut a piece of black cotton 4¾" × 5½". This is the coin
pocket. Turn the top edge under ¾" (Figure 6.23). Cut a
piece of Velcro 4¾" long; separate it. Center and sew the
soft section of the Velcro to the backside of the coin
pocket using two lines of satin stitching to reinforce this

Figure 6.20

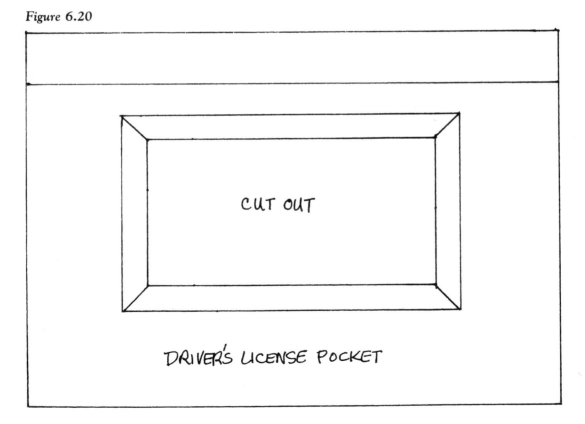

CUT OUT

DRIVER'S LICENSE POCKET

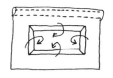

Figure 6.21

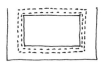

Figure 6.22

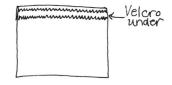

Figure 6.23

often-used pocket (Figure 6.24). Measure and mark 3½"
up from the bottom edge of the center inside panel. Center and sew the loop section of the Velcro in place.

10. Place the coin pocket flush with the bottom of the black
cotton inside panel (Figure 6.25) and then lay the driver's
license pocket flush with the bottom edge. Baste the pockets to the sides of the black cotton inside panel.

11. Cut two pieces of black cotton 3¾" × 5½". These will
make the four credit card pockets.

12. Take one piece and finger press the bottom edge under
¼" (Figure 6.26). Turn the top edge under ¼" twice and
edgestitch. Then sew another line of stitching ⅜" from the
top to catch the folded edge. Repeat for the other pocket.
Pin the pockets together, with the back pocket ⁵⁄₁₆" above
the other pocket (Figure 6.27). Lay the pockets on the
black cotton inside panel so the lower (top) pocket is flush
with the top edge of the coin pocket (Figure 6.28). Pin in
place at the top. Do not sew yet.

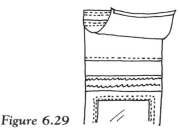

Velcro under

Figure 6.24

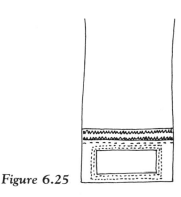

Figure 6.25

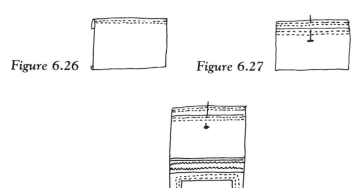

Figure 6.26

Figure 6.27

Figure 6.28

13. Lift up the top pocket. Sew the bottom of the higher (bottom) pocket in place (Figure 6.29). Flip down the top
credit card pocket and sew the bottom edge in place.

Figure 6.29

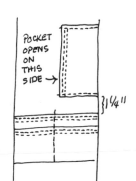

Figure 6.30

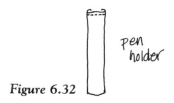

POCKET
OPENS
ON
THIS
SIDE →

$1\frac{1}{4}$"

Figure 6.31

pen
holder

Figure 6.32

Figure 6.33

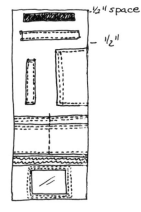

$\frac{1}{2}$" space

$\frac{1}{2}$"

Find the center and sew down the center of the two pockets to create four credit card pockets (Figure 6.30).

14. Cut a piece of black cotton 4" × 7". This is the checkbook pocket. Cut a piece of black cotton $1\frac{1}{2}$" × 6". This is the pen holder.

15. Take the checkbook pocket piece. Finger press the short sides under $\frac{1}{4}$". Turn one edge of the pocket under $\frac{1}{4}$" twice. This becomes the side opening of the pocket. Edgestitch the side opening edge, then sew a line of stitching $\frac{3}{8}$" away (Figure 6.31).

16. Place the checkbook pocket $1\frac{1}{4}$" up from the top edge of the credit card holder on the black cotton inside panel (Figure 6.31). Make sure it is flush with the right-hand edge of the panel.

17. Take the cotton that will be the pen holder. Finger press the long sides under $\frac{1}{4}$". Turn one short edge (the top) under $\frac{1}{4}$" twice and topstitch (Figure 6.32). Center the pen holder in the space to the left of the checkbook pocket on the inside panel. Place the topstitched edge toward the top of the panel. Edgestitch the pen holder in place (Figure 6.33).

18. Cut a piece of Ultraleather $1\frac{3}{4}$" × $5\frac{1}{2}$". This makes a sleeve for the bag handle. Fold the short ends under $\frac{1}{2}$", then fold the long sides under $\frac{1}{4}$". Place the sleeve $\frac{1}{2}$" up from the edge of the checkbook pocket (Figure 6.33). Center and sew the long edges to the black cotton inside panel.

19. Center and sew the other section of the Velcro piece that was sewn to the front panel $\frac{1}{2}$" down from the top edge of the black cotton inside panel (Figure 6.33).

20. Place the front and back cotton panels together, wrong sides facing. Cut a $1\frac{1}{2}$" strip of binding from the Ultraleather. Bind the edges of bag.

21. To finish the bag, feed the bag's cord through the sleeve on the inside of the wallet. Knot the ends together, and conceal the knot in sleeve.

⬤ UILTED ROSE BELT

With its single rose, this belt is great over long T-tops and sweaters (Figure 6.34).

MATERIALS

Chintz, old drapery fabric, or any medium-weight fabric printed
    with large flowers, ¼ yard for belt plus one rose cutout
Small piece of green cotton for leaves
¼ yard interfacing
3″ piece of ¾″-wide Velcro
Polyester fiberfill
Thread

Figure 6.34

PROCEDURE

1. This belt is made to size, although you will have a little
   leeway for those days when food is the spirit of the day.
   Measure your waist and add 2″ to the measurement. If
   your waist measures 27″, add 2″ to make 29″. Cut a 6″-
   wide piece of floral fabric to this measurement. Fuse the
   interfacing to the wrong side of the belt following the
   manufacturer's directions. Fold the belt in half lengthwise,
   right sides facing, and sew along the long edge, using a
   ⅝″ seam allowance. Turn right side out (Figure 6.35a).
   Center the seam in back and press. Fold short ends to the
   inside ½″ and topstitch around the entire belt. Set aside.

2. Pick one large flower from your fabric. A flower that isn't
   too intricate in shape works best. A rose is ideal, because it
   has a softly rounded outer edge. Cut out the flower, adding a ½″ seam allowance all around (Figure 6.35b). Cut a
   backing piece the same size. Place the flower and backing
   piece together, right sides facing, and sew all around ½″
   from the edge, leaving a 3″ opening for turning. Clip close
   to the seam and turn the piece right side out. Stuff the

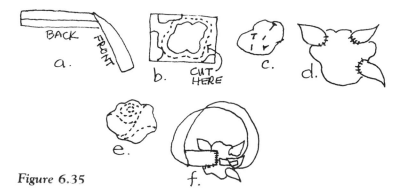

Figure 6.35

flower lightly with fiberfill and pin the opening to hold the stuffing in place (Figure 6.35c). Turn the raw edges to the inside and whipstitch the opening closed.

3. To quilt the flower, study the flower to determine where you want to add depth. The lighter areas should remain unquilted. If the flower has dark shadings, as does a rose, quilt these areas (Figure 6.35e). Set the quilted flower aside.

4. Cut the leaves from green cotton using the pattern in Figure 6.36. Place two leaves together, right sides facing, and sew together, leaving an opening for turning. Clip the seams and turn each leaf right side out. Stuff the leaves lightly with fiberfill and pin them to hold the stuffing in place. Turn raw edges under and whipstitch closed. Quilt the leaves as shown in Figure 6.37. Pin the quilted leaves in place on the back of the flower (Figure 6.35d). Be careful not to stitch through to the front of the rose.

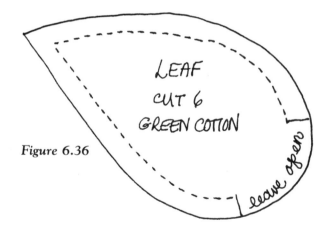

Figure 6.36

5. Center the belt ends, right sides facing, on the back of the flower. Stitch one end to the flower. Attach the fuzzy section of Velcro to the other side of the flower. Sew the looped piece of Velcro to the belt. To wear, simply put the belt around your waist, "buckling" it with the Velcro.

FLOWER GARDEN POCKET APRON

Since we never seem to have enough pockets, this is one answer (Figure 6.38). Try the Flower Garden Pocket Apron over a full folkloric skirt.

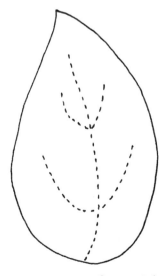

QUILTING PATTERN

Figure 6.37

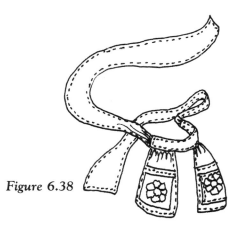

Figure 6.38

MATERIALS

1 yard printed heavy cotton fabric
¼ yard white cotton fabric
Small fabric scraps of six different prints
Thread

PROCEDURE

1. Cut out all pattern pieces (Figures 6.39, 6.40, 6.41, and 6.42). Pin them to the designated fabrics and cut out.
2. To construct the flower garden pockets, separate the hexagons into two piles. The center hexagon should be of the same print as the sash and banding. Place a hexagon on top of the center hexagon, right sides facing. Sew together along one edge, starting and stopping at the cross seam allowances. Open up the pieces. Lay the next hexagon on top of the center hexagon, right sides facing, and

Figure 6.39

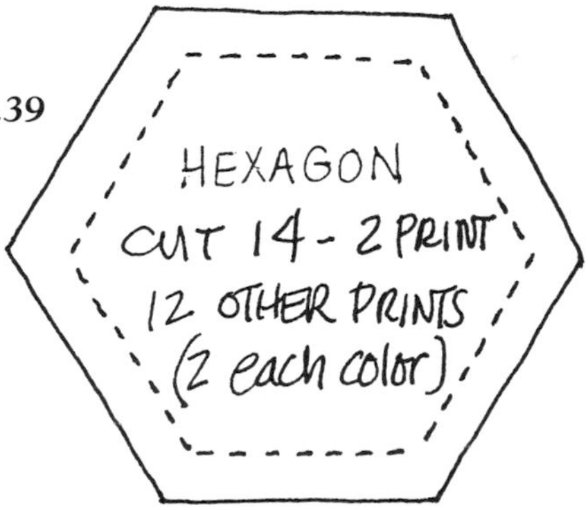

HEXAGON
CUT 14 - 2 PRINT
12 OTHER PRINTS
(2 each color)

Figure 6.40

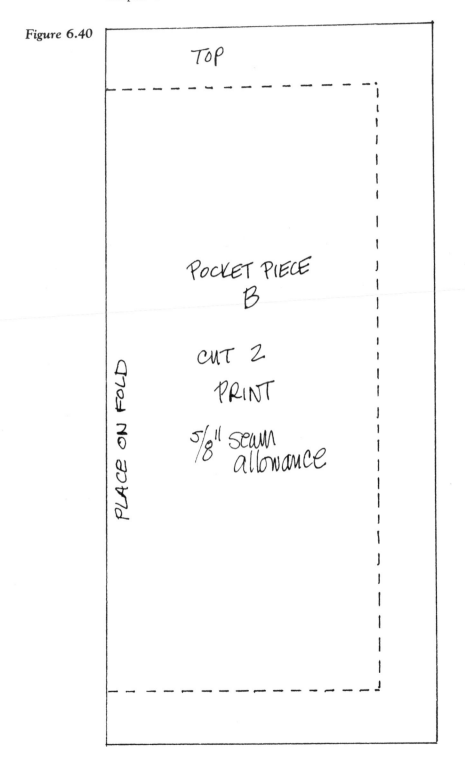

TOP

POCKET PIECE
B

CUT 2

PRINT

5/8" seam
allowance

PLACE ON FOLD

Figure 6.41

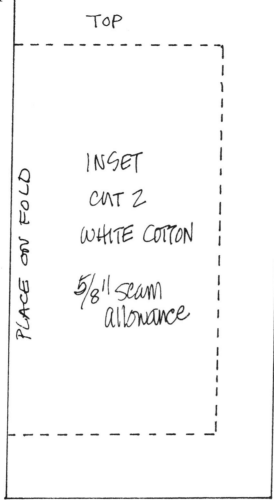

TOP

INSET

CUT 2

WHITE COTTON

5/8" seam
allowance

PLACE ON FOLD

sew along another edge, starting and stopping at the cross seam allowances. Repeat until all sides of the center hexagon have a piece sewn to them (Figure 6.43a). Place the right sides of the outer ring of hexagons together, each with its neighboring hexagon, and sew the ring together (Figure 6.43b). Construct the other flower garden piece the same way.

3. Turn the outside edges of the completed flower garden pieces under and press them so they hold. Center one of the flower garden pieces on one of the white cotton

Figure 6.42

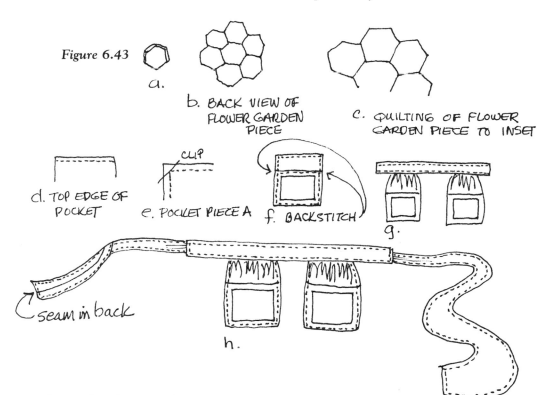

Figure 6.43

a.

b. BACK VIEW OF FLOWER GARDEN PIECE

c. QUILTING OF FLOWER GARDEN PIECE TO INSET

d. TOP EDGE OF POCKET

CLIP

e. POCKET PIECE A

f. BACKSTITCH

g.

seam in back

h.

insets. Sew in place along the outside edge, using a short quilting stitch (Figure 6.43c). Using the same stitch, sew ¼" outside the edge of the center hexagon. Turn the edges of the inset under ½" and press. Center the completed inset piece on Pocket Piece B. Sew in place (with your machine) ¼" from edge. Backstitch at the beginning and end of the stitching to hold it securely. Press the edges of Pocket Piece B under. Stitch across the top edge, using a ¼" seam allowance (Figure 6.43d). Repeat for the other pocket.

4. Place the two pieces of Pocket Piece A together, right sides facing, and sew all around it, leaving an opening at the top for turning. Clip across the corners and turn the piece right side out (Figure 6.43e). Press. Place Pocket Piece B on top of Pocket Piece A, lining up the bottom and sides. Pin. Stitch around the pockets ¼" from the edge, except at the top, which has been left open. Backstitch where the two pocket pieces join (Figure 6.43f). Baste the top edge of Pocket Piece A and gather. Set aside. Repeat for the other pocket.

5. From the print fabric, cut a waistband 4½" × 25" and two pieces for sashing, 5½" × 28" each. Fold the waistband in half, wrong sides facing. Press the raw edges under. Place gathered edge of each pocket in the pressed-under section, leaving a 3" space in between pockets (Figure 6.43g). Turn the short sides of the waistband to the inside and press. Pin to hold in place.

6. Fold one of the sashing pieces in half lengthwise, right sides facing. Sew along long edge. Turn right side out. Press so the seam is at the center back (Figure 6.43h). Turn the edges of one of the short ends to the inside. Pin in place. Topstitch ¼" from the edge all around leaving the raw end open. Gather the open end. Pin the sash in place in side opening of the waistband. Repeat for the other sash piece. Topstitch around the waistband, catching the sash pieces and pockets in stitching.

7. To wear the apron, place the band around your waist with the pockets in front and tie sashing in a big bow in the back.

A Final Word:
Keeping the Artistic Spirit Alive

Sometimes it's easier to turn on the TV and become a couch potato than to get started on that next piece of needle art. Most artists, especially those living in rural areas, work with little input and must continually motivate from within. However, there are a number of ways to break out of a rut or simply rebound from the hullabaloo of the holidays. Here are a few ways to recharge and find the joy of creating again.

Homage: Try out a new technique of someone you admire. Classes are available in most areas and books are accessible to everyone.

Explore: Is there an aspect of your work that needs refinement? Try new colors, lines, shapes, or forms. Wake up to fresh approaches.

Read: Go to your local library and spend the day going through the stacks. Try art (600s in the Dewey Decimal system), crafts/needlework (700s), and costume (300s). Don't forget to look in *Books in Print* and pamphlet files; try Interlibrary Loan.

Review: Look back through your work and assess the strengths and weaknesses. Find the best and stress it.

Cycle: Perhaps you work with more ease at certain times of the year. Personally, summer is my downtime. I grew up in a resort town and summer meant the beach. I've learned not to fight it. Summer is still the beach and catching up on fiction and other reading not related to my work. (Although I always carry a sketchbook to capture an idea!)

Rework: Take one idea and interpret it as many times as possible to exhaust the possibilities. Change threads and textures; incorporate unusual materials.

Observe: Spend a day in a large city or town observing streetwear. Seek out the outré areas, colleges, the working class, and ethnic communities.

Subscribe: Keep the information line open. Each magazine has a slightly different slant.

Multimedia: Try painting and writing. Solve problems in a different medium.

Don't try too hard or it will show in your work. Relax. Your muse will be back.

If you would like to share an idea or comment, write to me:

Linda Fry Kenzle
P.O. Box 177
Fox River Grove, IL 60021

Some of the ideas may be used in a future book. You will be given full credit.

Are you interested in a quarterly newsletter about creative uses of the sewing machine, serger, and knitting machine? Write to The Creative Machine, P.O. Box 2634, Menlo Park, CA 94026.

Resources

Suppliers

Aardvark Territorial Enterprise
P.O. Box 2449
Livermore, CA 94550
Lively newspaper/catalog of unusual notions and doodads; sample copy $2.00

Angelsea
P.O. Box 4586
Stockton, CA 95204
Extensive line of beautiful ribbons and laces; catalog $3.00, refundable

ARC
471 East 124th Avenue
Denver, CO 80241
Threads, backings, etc.

Bead Art
60 North Court Street
Athens, OH 45701
Full line of beads, Fimo, beading supplies

BeadZip
2316 Sarah Lane
Falls Church, VA 22043
Unusual beads from around the world; catalog $5.00, refundable

Blueprint-Printables
1504 #7 Industrial Way
Belmont, CA 94002
Line of clothing in cotton, rayon or silk ready for you to paint and embellish, blueprint cloth, and T-shirts; catalog $3.00

Cerulean Blue, Ltd.
P.O. Box 21168
Seattle, WA 98111-3168
Procion dyes, fabric paint, chemicals, SureStamp for making stencils, silk painting supplies

Clotilde
1909 Southwest First Avenue
Fort Lauderdale, FL 33315-2100
Special sewing machine feet, pleater, and much more

Craft Gallery
P.O. Box 145
Swampscott, MA 01907
Books and supplies for all genres of needlework

Danforth Pewterers
P.O. Box 828
Middlebury, VT 05753
Pewter buttons and pins

Dharma Trading Company
P.O. Box 150916
San Rafael, CA 94915
Paints, blank clothing

Dogwood Lane
P.O. Box 145
Dugger, IN 47848
Ceramic and porcelain buttons finished or available as blanks that you paint and glaze yourself, frayed clothing patterns

Donna Sayler's Fabulous Furs
700 Madison Avenue
Covington, KY 41011
Kits for faux furs, Ultraleather; catalog $1.00

Earth Guild
33 Haywood Street
Asheville, NC 28811
Dyes, Deka paint, weaving supplies, Fimo, Sculpey III, books, marbling kits

Elsie's Exquisiques
P.O. Box 260
208 State Street
St. Joseph, MI 49085
Ribbons, rosettes, trim, tassels, and fringe

Freed Company
P.O. Box 394
Albuquerque, NM 87103
Semiprecious beads, sequin appliqués, feed bags (all in large quantities)

Friends Patterns
P.O. Box 1753
Homestead, FL 33030-1753
Patterns for swimwear and exercise clothing

Gardin' of Beadin'
P.O. Box 1535
Redway, CA 95560
Unusual beads, books, supplies

Green Pepper
3918 West First Avenue
Eugene, OR 97402
Outdoor clothing patterns and accessories; catalog $2.00

Japanese Embroidery Center
Kurenai-Kai, Ltd.
2727 Spalding Drive
Dunwoody, GA 30350
Japanese threads

Keepsake Quilting
Dover Street
P.O. Box 1459
Meredith, NH 03253-1459
Everything for quilting

Kuma
Box 2712
Glenville, NY 12325
Beads and supplies

Lacis
2982 Adeline Street
Berkeley, CA 94703
Patterns, lace making supplies, reproduction sewing accessories

Michel Ferre Silks
P.O. Box 958
Niwot, CO 80544
Exquisite silks; catalog $12.00, refundable with first order

National Thread and Supply Co.
695 Red Oak Road
Stockbridge, GA 30281
Threads galore, notions, garment racks for doing shows

Optional Extras, Inc.
150A Church Street
Burlington, VT 05401
Bead and jewelry supplies, Fimo, Sculpey III; color catalog $2.50

Photographer's Formulary
P.O. Box 950
Condon, MT 59826
Blueprinting and brownprinting kits

Promenade Enterprises, Inc.
P.O. Box 2092
Boulder, CO 80306-2092
Beads

Rainshed
707 Northwest 11th Avenue
Corvalis, OR 97330
Patterns and fabrics for outdoor clothing and accessories

Rainy Day Patterns
P.O. Box 5469
Eugene, OR 97405
Appliqué patterns

Rockland Colloid Corporation
302 Piermont Avenue
Piermont, NY 10968
Photographic transfer supplies

Rupert, Gibbon and Spider, Inc.
P.O. Box 425
Healdsburg, CA 95448
Paint, chemicals for fabric, marbling supplies

Sax Arts and Crafts
P.O. Box 51710
New Berlin, WI 53151-1710
Huge color catalog of everything for artists and crafters

Shipwreck Beads
5021 Mud Bay Road
Olympia, WA 98502
Beads, books, 527 cement; catalog $3.00; minimum order $25.00

Swanco Industrial, Inc.
1425 South Allec Street
Anaheim, CA 92805
Design Dye

Testfabrics, Inc.
P.O. Box 420
Middlesex, NJ 08846
All types of fabric for painters, dyers, embellishers

TSI, Inc.
P.O. Box 9266
Seattle, WA 98109
Fimo, Sculpey III, gold, silver, findings

Westcroft Beadworks, Inc.
139 Washington Street
Norwalk, CT 06854
Excellent color catalog of beads; minimum order $50.00

YLI
P.O. Box 109
Provo, UT 84603-0109
Silk ribbon and unusual thread; catalog $1.50

Periodicals

American Quilter
(The American Quilter's
Society)
5801 Kentucky Dam Road
Paducah, KY 42001

Creative Machine Newsletter
P.O. Box 2634
Menlo Park, CA 94026

Creative Needle
Box 99
Lookout Mountain, TN
37350

*Ink & Gall: The Marbling
Journal*
P.O. Box 1469
Taos, NM 87571

Lace and Crafts
3201 East Lakeshore Drive
Tallahasse, FL 32312-2034

Ornament
P.O. Box 2349
San Marcos, CA 92079-2349

Piecework
201 East Fourth Street
Loveland, CO 80537

Sew Beautiful
518 Madison Street
Huntsville, AL 35801

Sew News
News Plaza
P.O. Box 1790
Peoria, IL 61656

Surface Design Association
P.O. Box 20799
Oakland, CA 94620

Threads
63 South Main Street
Newton, CT 06470

Bibliography

Anderson, Kay, *Fashion with Ribbons*, Batsford, London, 1987.

Anscombe, Isabella, *A Woman's Touch*, Penguin Books, New York, 1985.

Art and Craft of Ribbonwork, The, Body Blueprints, Mill Valley, CA, 1987.

Avery, Virginia, *Quilts to Wear*, Charles Schribner's Sons, New York, 1987.

Barber, Vicki, and Tessa Bird, *The Fine Art of Quilting*, E. P. Dutton, New York, 1988.

Bell, Quentin, *On Human Finery*, Schocken, New York, 1976.

Bennett, d.j., *Machine Embroidery with Style*, Madrona Publishers, Seattle, 1980.

Best, Muriel, *Stumpwork*, Batsford, London, 1987.

Black, Mary E., *Key to Weaving*, Bruce, Milwaukee, 1945.

Bowman, Sara, *A Fashion for Extravagance*, E. P. Dutton, New York, 1985.

Chung, Young Y., *The Art of Oriental Embroidery*, Charles Schribner's Sons, New York, 1979.

Complete Guide to Needlework, Reader's Digest Press, Pleasantville, NY, 1979.

Creative Sewing Ideas, Cy DeCosse, Minnetonka, MN, 1990.

Davis, Marian L., *Visual Design in Dress*, Prentice-Hall, New York, 1987.

Designs by Erté, Dover, New York, 1976.

Dodson, Jackie, *How to Make Soft Jewelry*, Chilton, Radnor, PA, 1991.

Edwards, Betty, *Drawing on the Artist Within*, Simon & Schuster, New York, 1986.

Ekiguchi, Kunio, *Gift Wrapping*, Kodanska International, Tokyo, 1985.

Ericson, Lois, *Fabrics . . . Reconstructed*, Eric's Press, Salem, OR, 1985.

e Physics and C
icago, 1986.
elma, Quiltir
n Publishers,
nhardt, Heidi, A
9.
ichard M., and Jennife.
versity of Washington Pre.
Jane, Frame Loom Weaving, V
, 1984.
s, Comfort Clothes, Celestial Arts, M
Zandra, and Anne Knight, The Art of Zan
ughton Mifflin, Boston, 1985.
rt Publishing, Old-Fashioned Ribbonwork, Do
, 1988.
an, The New Clay, Flower Valley Press, Rockville,
1.
loe, Costumes of Mexico, University of Texas Press,
stin, 1985.
t, Margaret, A Basic Textile Book, Van Nostrand Reinhold,
w York, 1975.
obert, The Anatomy of Costume, Crescent, New York,
77.
Penny, Functions of Dress, Prentice-Hall, Englewood Cliffs,
, 1987.
Vance, Making Artist's Tools, Van Nostrand Reinhold,
w York, 1979.
Elyse, and Mike Summer, Wearable Crafts, Crown, New
rk, 1976.
ay, The Batsford Book of Embroidery Techniques, Batsford,
ndon, 1984.
son, Sue, Decorative Dressmaking, Rodale, Emmaus, PA,
85.
Max, Costume Patterns and Designs, Hastings House, New
ork, 1974.
, Leo, What Is Art? translated by Aylmer Maude,
Macmillan, New York, 1960.
h, Janet, Working Wardrobe, Acropolis Books, Washington,
C, 1981.
Jean, A Patchworthy Apparel Book, Yours Truly, Westminster,
A, n.d.
, Jean, Joinings, Edges, and Trims, Van Nostrand Reinhold
New York, 1983.

Ericson, Nina, K
Evans, Ann, C
1986.
Fanning, Rob
Quiltir
Fanning, R
Eml
The Fibe
Fitch,

Fjels

Fo
E

A Note on Metrics

The following two lists will help you convert measurements given in this book in inches and yards to centimeters (cm) and meters (m). For piece work, make sure that the sum of the parts of the project equal the total measurement. Add your conversion measurements together and adjust them if they don't equal the conversion for the total amount.

1 inch = 2.54 centimeters exactly. These measurements are rounded to the nearest .5 centimeter.

⅛ in.	= 3 mm	9 in.	= 23 cm	29 in.	= 73.5 cm
¼ in.	= 6 mm	10 in.	= 25.5 cm	30 in.	= 76 cm
⅜ in.	= 1 cm	11 in.	= 28 cm	31 in.	= 78.5 cm
½ in.	= 1.3 cm	12 in.	= 30.5 cm	32 in.	= 81.5 cm
⅝ in.	= 1.5 cm	13 in.	= 33 cm	33 in.	= 84 cm
¾ in.	= 2 cm	14 in.	= 35.5 cm	34 in.	= 86.5 cm
1 in.	= 2.5 cm	15 in.	= 38 cm	35 in.	= 89 cm
1¼ in.	= 3 cm	16 in.	= 40.5 cm	36 in.	= 91.5 cm
1½ in.	= 4 cm	17 in.	= 43 cm	37 in.	= 94 cm
2 in.	= 5 cm	18 in.	= 45.5 cm	38 in.	= 96.5 cm
2½ in.	= 6.5 cm	19 in.	= 48.5 cm	39 in.	= 99 cm
3 in.	= 7.5 cm	20 in.	= 51 cm	40 in.	= 101.5 cm
3½ in.	= 9 cm	21 in.	= 53.5 cm	41 in.	= 104 cm
4 in.	= 10 cm	22 in.	= 56 cm	42 in.	= 106.5 cm
4½ in.	= 11.5 cm	23 in.	= 58.5 cm	43 in.	= 109 cm
5 in.	= 12.5 cm	24 in.	= 61 cm	44 in.	= 112 cm
5½ in.	= 14 cm	25 in.	= 63.5 cm	45 in.	= 114.5 cm
6 in.	= 15 cm	26 in.	= 66 cm	46 in.	= 117 cm
7 in.	= 18 cm	27 in.	= 68.5 cm	47 in.	= 119.5 cm
8 in.	= 20.5 cm	28 in.	= 71 cm		

A *Note on Metrics*

1 yard = .9144 meter exactly. These measurements are rounded
to the nearest .01 meter and .5 centimeter, respectively.

⅛ yd.	= .12 m	= 11.5 cm		1 yd.	= .92 m	= 91.5 cm
¼ yd.	= .23 m	= 23 cm		1¼ yd.	= 1.15 m	= 114.5 cm
⅜ yd.	= .35 m	= 34.5 cm		1½ yd.	= 1.38 m	= 137 cm
½ yd.	= .46 m	= 46 cm		1¾ yd.	= 1.61 m	= 160 cm
⅝ yd.	= .57 m	= 57 cm		2 yd.	= 1.84 m	= 183 cm
¾ yd.	= .69 m	= 68.5 cm		3 yd.	= 2.76 m	= 274.5 cm
⅞ yd.	= .80 m	= 80 cm				

Index